EXILED TO EARTH

Other books by Van Heyden

Conquering Things

Poetry My Mother Would've Approved

Poetry Even Your Mother Would Approve

Poetry My Mother Would Not Have Approved

What Kids Know That Adults Have Forgot

On Conquering Things

The Reincarnation of Edgar Allan Poe

VELVET GLOVES PUBLISHING
© 2015

Nashville, TN
www.velvetglovespub.com
All RIGHTS RESERVED

1st Printing June 2015
2nd Printing April 2017

Here is a very well-paced novel with real as dirt characters in a Sci-Fi contemporary setting.

Turn the page for outstanding reviews.

"Very original in his form and brilliant in the delivery of his message. A spiritual message I would say, that reminds one to don't give up on looking for the truth and the reasons of existence as a spiritual being.

A book that will make you smile and think about life and rekindle questions that you may have forgotten with the age or lost it in the day to day existence. A well-paced story with an oriental touch at the end." – L. B.

"An unusual and interesting book that keeps your attention to the end. Elvis is a delightful character, infused with mega personality and great humor. One to add to your 'must read' list. Van Heyden is an excellent author." Author – F. Botham

"I'm so busy that I rarely read a book from cover to cover and figured I'd do the same with this one. But I was so fascinated by *EXILED TO EARTH* that I kept coming back to it night after night, squeezing it in and enjoying every adventure, on the edge of my chair on what's going to be happening next. -- D. Sanders

"I just read this book *EXILED TO EARTH* by Chaz Van Heyden. I found it captivating and full of intrigue! It kept my interest all the way through and had lots of plausible Sci-Fi, mystical, spiritual amenities wrapped up with enough mystery plus suspense that really gets one thinking with the character and seeing life on Earth from his eyes as a foreigner to earth.

There is plenty of story line...and gets you as the reader thinking. I really was captivated by the story! Makes you wonder what if it were true." – CMJ

"This is a fascinating look at the "inside/outside" process of discovering who you used to be and how that influences who you are today. Elvis uses inside, earthly processes such as séances, martial arts, travelling and spiritual nourishment to reach out to the world he formerly existed in and to discover how he came to be marooned here on earth. This means fully connecting with his fellow space traveler Joshua and with all of the more mundane humans he comes into contact with here on Earth."
– J. Ianni

We live under the shadow of a gigantic question mark. Who are we? Where do we come from? Whither are we bound? – Hendrik Willem Van Loon *The Story of Man*

CONTENTS

CONTENTS

PART III   SELLIER

ENVOI

To
All those who yearn
To know their true
Identity

C. Van Heyden

EXILED TO EARTH

PART I

DISCOVERY AND VOW

C. Van Heyden

-

EXILED TO EARTH

These are the confessions of Elvis Apolliani, as told to Joshua Micah, a lay minister, and compiled later by a friend of the alien (narrator).

Confessee:

I didn't originate from Earth. But that was something I didn't know until later in my life. I want these confessions recorded so that if something happens to me it will be known why.

Being born human, was like many of my experiences not pleasant. I do remember being tugged out of a moist, slippery but very constrictive body, my mother, and held up in a glaring light by a white-coated mild mannered man who then slapped my bottom smartly a couple of times. At the time I thought, "Is this all there is to the initiation rite?"

Bye and bye I was fed some interesting cocktail from my mother's feeding apparatus, and then promptly to sleep.

Next image is of a small jail cell with no roof.

Every time I opened my mouth to speak a squawk

would come out. Therefore, I stopped opening my mouth, except for more cocktail, which it seemed the body that I was inhabiting liked and wanted ever so much.

In time my physical form got larger and more powerful, and I could get around the enclosure and even out if I cared to.

Once ambulatory, I plotted my complete escape.

EXILED TO EARTH

BULLIES & HASHISH

C. Van Heyden

All the years intervening between school and the jailhouse were…boring and pretty much meaningless. It was when I met Christopher that I got interested. He lived in a fabulously outfitted house in the swankiest spot in Manhattan, with chandeliers and sumptuous curving balustrades, and plenty of highly polished marble floors. This I reveled in. And the party food was just as bodacious.

Unfortunately, it didn't last because my ding-bat mother moved me and some other aliens to the suburbs. Cruelty, *the kind* I had never experienced before. I thought.

The first thing I did when I got to our new home was, I went up on the roof and rained down rocks and anything else solid on the strangers below, seventy feet below. That was when I was five. First confession.

The one thing my mother did, that was not stupid, was to name me Elvis. But when she did, it was a two edged sword. Girls loved me, not just because of my name but I also could dance and liked to dance with them. The guys on the other hand wanted to pick fights, a lot. One fight, that should have been stopped before it got too far, was with a guy named Roland, a kind of bully, and with a mean streak that I've never seen since in another human. He threatened me one day after school, and I had no escape this time, but I was ready for him because I knew the kind of character he was, so I had hidden a pair of brass knuckles in my back pocket and told no one. I didn't wait for him to kick me or wrestle me to the ground and then sit on me, as was his habit, I just turned my back to him and as I whirled away from his sight brought out the knuckles slipped them on my right hand, and as I came 360 launched a blow right below his left ear and down he went, and out. That was fine with me, because some of his gang buddies were there. When they saw what happened and so suddenly and that he was a goner they eased away from me and I headed out down the street. Confession #2.

"Hey Sal, how long before this methedrine kicks in?" It was about nine o'clock at night.

"Walk around a little and it will." Sal, was a jock in my high school but I got him started on MJ. Now he was upping the ante so I had to go along. We downed it in a place called Woodsdale, noted for its close but sequestered location away from the city. I had to admire him, he was a specimen of good strength, physique, body tone, and without his spectacles not a bad looking guy. All this was due to diligent weight lifting and calisthenics.

Here's what happened that night: we went our separate ways in a forest area that had few visitors. I started gabbing to myself and felt at the same time my blood racing, and my skin becoming unusually sensitive to the slight breeze. Shortly I found myself naked and luxuriating in what I thought was a sexual experience. I had removed my clothes, and feeling yet warm I continued walking around…and around, and around, until finally I just had to take a D-U-M-P. I'm naked, out in the open but where my clothes are I don't know, and now I'm paranoid about taking one. So, I search for a hidden place. Then it gets serious. I also don't know my way back to the cabin, it's after ten o'clock and I'm still thinking I've got to find a hidden place. Just when it's most critical I see it. It's a tent, nice tent and it looks uninhabited—a little low for my six foot plus body. When I'm done I get out of there, just in case, and head north where I will rendezvous with Sal no doubt. Confession # 3

But it starts to rain. This turns out to be a blessing because it is a warm, gentle, titillating rain that increases the pleasure of my walk-around in nature. Hours later I bump into the path I started out on and make my way into the cabin. It's 3:00 am. Sal comes in a few minutes later, there's a fire going and two large high-back chairs, perfect. We sit and jabber at each other for another hour or two, going faster than a roller-coaster writing our next two novels verbally to each other, and laughing a lot about it as it's happening.

Somehow, I found my clothes and put them on. Sal told me, same thing happened to him. Except the part about the dump.

My mother and I had only a few talks about sex. She seemed distant when I brought it up. I didn't tell her anything about "Jane" the girl who was obsessed over me. I just threw out a couple of harmless questions like, "Is it against our religion to have sex with a girl if we're not married?" She was quick to tell me about statutory rape, whatever that was. Later I learned what it meant, but the word rape came in there so strong I stopped asking about that. What if the girl desired it more than I did, was my next question, or would have been. My dad wasn't and hadn't been around for many years. It was so odd being secretly afraid of my mother finding out I had magazines with pictures of naked and semi-naked women and girls in them; when at the same time any summer there were dozens of girls who were wearing practically nothing and often would let slip a string here or there.

There's this girl that digs me while I'm in H.S. but I don't dig her. I don't know why I don't dig her, I just don't. We go out with friends, and a couple of parties, and it...we just don't click at all, not even a little. I learn the more I try and get away from somebody who likes me the harder it is. I hurt her feelings. Another time, I'm at one of the parties, I'm taking a pee in the rest room with no door, and another girl walks in on me, and says "Oops". Then the same girl later tries to ignore me turning her back on me, I say "That's OK, I prefer seeing your back to the front." I got for the first time the feeling that I was an alien of some sort."

"Well I guess that's all for today, did you get it all down, Josh?"

"All of it." When do you want to get together again?

"I don't know, but soon because lots of things are boiling over in my head."

C. Van Heyden

MILITARY SERVICE & THE SHOCK

C. Van Heyden

When it came time for me to register for the draft I thought, 'Not this war!' In the back of my head, something very familiar about young men being dragged off to some conflict very distant from their homes. I talked to a lot of guys. Some were running across the border, some were getting married quick, and some had the guts to go into the pre-induction physical with all sorts of tricks. I had one, I had been saving it up for just such a confrontation: I could roll my eyes completely up into my head so that only the whites showed and keep them there indefinitely. I did this nonchalantly and with no warning. This scared the examining doctor who, after having tested me positive for drugs, immediately wrote down, *not suitable for military training.*

But I wasn't done. Before I could get off the base, two rather ugly uniformed men, maybe sergeants came up to me and tried to make me join. They had me pinioned between them and were pressing the air out of my lungs. I rolled my eyes and they stopped squeezing the life out of me, long enough for me to tell them that I have syphilis, and I'd bite them if they try that again.

C. Van Heyden

Normally my height scares most guys away or puts doubt in their minds about trying to overpower me.

One day I'm tooling along the boardwalk, and I meet YOU, you remember that day, right?

"Never forget it." (Josh got a little uneasy.)

"You stared at me for about five minutes, and I was freaking out."

"It didn't seem five minutes *to me*. More like five light years. I was getting sick, and I was almost falling down, then you came over and said, 'what's the gig?'", and I still couldn't speak I was so bad off. Here's sort of a confession: that night I had a very bad dream, and the gist of that dream is of being put in a box, a metal box and shot into space. It kept repeating and repeating all night, and I could feel the coldness of space and the shriek of the metal box as it slid out of the atmosphere. Finally, in the morning exhausted and wet, I lay in my wet sheets and came to the conclusion that I'm not from Earth, I was born here on Earth, but I'm from somewhere else.

To astute readers: Josh studied his friend closely for a minute. He didn't laugh or even snicker, to do so would be a violation of his vows; but, listening to me talk and confess, Josh was himself strangely affected by the things I was saying.

"Is anyone else aware of this?", asked Josh.

"If you mean my being from another galaxy, no. I did mention the bad dream to some friends."

"Did you get an image of your shape in the metal box?"

"Not really because I was wrapped in something very tight like a mummy. There wasn't any light."

"Any idea from where or why?" I could point to the area of the sky, but how far I can't decide.

"Why?"

Elvis thought, 'Because I had done, or was accused of horrible things.

Joshua waited silently.... "I was accused of assassinating a government official. I was accused of raping his wife."

"You were exiled then?"

"I was exiled, but when I saw you for the first time on the boardwalk, I only sensed I knew you."

"And who am I to you?"

"Your name then was Amtar, and you too were sent off to Earth like I was. You don't recollect? "

"None whatsoever."

"You will."

NIGHTMARE REALITY

C. Van Heyden

That night a dream. In it I saw myself changing shapes. One shape, that of a falcon. And I saw the ground way below and wings to either side and I could also feel the air rushing by. And soon I was in the chamber of the dead man's wife. It was unclear whether she was alone or what her features were, nonetheless I knew where I was and who she was.

"You are the one who took my husband's life!" rang out of the hazy scene.

"Only because you said you were tired of him," came the retort. "But it was a fair fight. I took his life fairly and in defense of my own life – he attacked me first."

"So, he knew of our affair?"

"Quite so, and for some time apparently, enough so that it made him angry bitter and hateful towards me, but not towards you."

"That's true, Marquez grew indifferent about sex and on the other hand my needs increased. "How shall we escape punishment if there were no witnesses?"

"I have planted the bludgeon in your brother's room in his closet. This they will find, and with the knowledge of his obsessive love for you they will not execute him but exile him only."

I sprang out of the dream choking with emotion. I had been sent to Earth as punishment for a crime I had not committed, even the incest never happened. But what most aggrieved me was the fact that at one time I possessed powers to change beingness at will.

"If I could get back that power...." This one thought became my obsession.

.....

Across town Joshua was telling a friend about, but not the details of Elvis's confession: "You're gonna laugh when I tell you this, but I've taken on a fellow who believes he's an alien sent to Earth as punishment."

"Is he from California?" The undergraduate, James, thought it best to tie it into the old joke about Californians being the whackiest bunch around, what with their constant food fads, and UFO group meetings at Big Rock, and all that. Wasn't Aldous Huxley born in Los Angeles, home of the dingbats.

"It's not that simple, James, this guy remembers in more detail the more he confesses."

"Well, write a book about it then, but change the

names to protect the 'innocent' and it should be a huge Fantasy story success."

"Are you familiar with the kings of Egypt?"

"Not something I studied so far."

"Well, would it interest you to know that they most profoundly believed in previous existences?" In fact, the whole meaning of the Egyptian Book of the Dead is about the coming forth the day after entombment and progressing either to another life or to a place in the constellations."

"That's pretty interesting."

Meanwhile, Elvis was himself dwelling on the very topic of ancient Egypt. He remembered how real were the black and white films of the '50's, about the mummy and tombs of the pharaohs. Only now he was recalling a certain deed of his that made him cringe.

'On no, I couldn't have been that evil' The thought pierced his mind. 'And I see myself cutting the hands off a man, and blinding him too.'

'What act could, by another, have justified such cruelty?' And Elvis concluded that it was only cruelty that he was viewing, his cruelty.

C. Van Heyden

"I have to tell Joshua this happened." And as these words fell from his mouth it became quite clear, alarmingly clear, that he had dismembered and blinded Joshua in a previous existence.

SÉANCES & IMAGES
FROM THE PAST

C. Van Heyden

Elvis had a calendar, a most beautiful Chinese calendar book, with illustrations opposite each day diary. The illustrations were pictures of Chinese pagodas, temples, mountain retreats, forests, glades and waterfalls. The giant pagodas being the most impressive. He felt strongly attracted to these pictures almost to the level of adoration. He now wondered, "Is this why earthlings get so unreasonably attached to objects and images?"

He remembered the anguish he felt when reading in elementary school 'The Good Earth'. It was the most agonizingly long and unending travail of one family. Wang Lung, the principle character, was at once completely real but completely repulsive. The more he studied the pictures the easier it was for Elvis to recall his lives he spent in China.

He knew with complete certainty that he had been a bandit, several lives. It was an easy life compared to a serf, until caught. Elvis also glimpsed the many opium sessions, in fact thousands he had either attended or constructed for his friends and village-mates: this being the only way to escape the intolerable condition of being a peasant.

Later that day he met with Joshua and told him of his exploits in banditry, the robberies of government emissaries and caravans of private goods, the killing of guards and watchmen, all necessary to success. He went easy on the rape of women since this was still a sore subject. But to himself he was enlightened as to his current state and sentiments in that regard.

By the time Elvis was through confessing, Joshua was about to confess himself that he had divulged the nature of these sessions to James, and likely James will find out his identity. But Joshua didn't.

Elvis had a vague but nagging notion that since China he had also not been a "good boy." And maybe he could do something about that. It could happen that he might get back some if not all his powers and use them to make life for others more comfortable even satisfying, wouldn't that make up for all the evil he had perpetrated? Then the thought occurred to him, I've got it backwards, if I make every effort to make life better for others, then I *will be rewarded* with a return of my powers. But first he must discover the true nature of where he came from.

Elvis picked up a tabloid type newspaper, one of many he perused and in the back in the classifieds it read, "Want to know the truth about who you really are? Want to communicate with deceased loved ones? Séance with Madame Chartreuse at 9:00 PM. 1220 Aberdeen St. Telephone ahead for seating. Limited space."

The night of the session with Madame Chartreuse was a howling success: not only did Elvis get to talk with the deceased but he also found out about his home planet.

"Madame C., will you call up my friend 'Amtar'?"

"Certainly that should be easy." How close of a friend is this Amtar?"
"Oh, we've been through many battles together"

"I see, and when did you last see him, I take it 'Amtar' is a man?"

"Oh, that definitely, although not to be cryptic, he may have been a woman also, if you get my drift?"

"Amtar, whether man or woman come now to us and speak the truth here in this hallowed gathering," invoked the séancer.

If Elvis now heard a voice other than Joshua's he knew this was a hoax. The silent audience waited. Minutes went by but not a word was spoken or heard. Again Madame C. called for an answer. Expressions all around the sitting room varied from bewilderment to sly smiles. Unflustered Madame C. asked, "how long has Amtar been dead?"

"Many years now, many, many years."

And then Madame C. said something truly wonderful: "This Amtar is here on Earth now, but he goes by another name."

This electrified some of the participants, but not Elvis; this was precisely the answer he was looking to hear.

"That is correct, Madame C. Are you familiar with Egyptian mythology at all?"

"Yes quite, it has been in my lineage, and is where we derive our spiritual skills."

"Very good then, and perhaps, Madame C. you can discover from what planet Amtar came?"

"He didn't come from any one planet, but the last one before Earth was Sellier."

"Could you please show us or tell us where 'Sellier' is located?" "Certainly," and she raised her arm and pointed in the direction Elvis would have pointed, the place where he had come from.

Then Elvis deferred to another guest who was visibly gladdened there was truth in Madame Chartreuse's séance. "Could I speak with my lost brother at sea, Martin?" Again, Madame C. invoked the spirits last known name, and again, but not as long awaited a sound or signal a connection had been made.

Faintly then a weak voice, like that of a feeble old man was heard, "Who calls me"?

"It is your brother who still lives and loves you, and misses you dearly," spoke the brother.

"Matthew?" And the brother answered, "Yes, I'm alive but you were lost to us when your ship blew up and sank."

"I am cold, very cold and alone. I died?"

"Yes, and I and my wife grieved for you, until tonight."

"Then I am dead, that's what happened."

"There were no survivors. But we are so glad now to know that you are not eternally dead."

"Where shall I go, what shall I do?"

"Oh, my dear brother, that I cannot decide."

Then Elvis asked if he could say a word to Martin. And his brother nodding assent, Elvis asked, "Why not come back to Earth and try again?"

The feeble voice, audibly stronger replied, "If I could just find out where I am and where Earth is…"

Then Madame C. called to Martin, "Do you see any lights any white spots around you?"

"Yes faintly, there are some." "All right then pick out the one that you associate with our voices…did you do that?"

"I think I see one over there to the right." "Good. Be where it is."

"I see only shadows…" All right, that's fine. Now be near Earth." For minutes Martin did not communicate. Then, "I see a planet or something like it. I feel a pull towards it."

"Excellent. Now, locate a maternity ward."

A few minutes passed. Then the sound of a baby crying. Then silence.

Madame C. declared, "Martin has been reborn. I should like to end the séance."

All present agreed.

C. Van Heyden

POWERS REVIVE

C. Van Heyden

Elvis made a pact with himself that he would use Madame Chartreuse again, and the next time he wouldn't stop interrogating her until he found out how he was transported to Earth, she did say she was well versed in Egyptian mythology, which was their ancient religion as well.

It was about this time that one of Elvis' latent powers revivified. This occurrence so edified him at once that he vowed he would lead a much more altruistic life. No sooner than he made his vow, he was confronted with a test of his will.

James, the student whose confidence Joshua had trusted, was telling everyone he could on campus about Elvis. It would have been justifiable to smash James in the face. But Elvis, knowing that violence begets violence, just dropped the matter. What did he care really what a bunch of earthlings thought about him. Plus, he'd made his vow, and that was sacred. He didn't even mention it to Joshua when they met for their next session.

"What did you find out at the séance?" Joshua started off, before calling the session formally to order.

"Well it was interesting, I got to talk to a man who apparently died in a ship disaster, and Madame

Chartreuse, as she calls herself, confirmed the existence of planet named Sellier in the direct line that I had pointed to the other night."

"Did it jog your memory more, like it had before?"

"Didn't jog, but it did confirm that one, I did come from a distant civilization and two, Madame C. as I'll call her, is no sham. She's got some abilities most don't."

"The last thing we were talking about was the banditry in China…"

"That's right, in China. There were similar bandits in India, they were called thugees. Luring caravans with riches into traveling with them for protection but then turning on their guests at the first opportunity, usually killing them. I believe I have counted the number to myself who I personally dispatched and I am content with that as my confession."

"Where do we go from here?" inquired Joshua.

"Well, there's isn't much coming up anymore in China or Asia for that matter. Remember, most lives lived in that time period were that of peasant farmers."

"So, you don't have anything you want to tell me?"

"Oh…no, that's not it, I want to make a pact that we never let ourselves be cruel to, or try not to be cruel to others. See I believe that that is a key to why earthlings are trapped—well we are all somewhat trapped here, aren't we?"

"You know, I have to tell you that you should make that pact with Jesus, he's the one who can see you through those times better than I."

"I'd like to do that, but you know, I just can't get over the fact that Jesus had such terrific powers, but he lost sometimes control of them, see? And, he got himself crucified. That was his only big mistake. Most don't want to follow in his path because it's just too painful, the more you try to be like Jesus the more you get scourged in this world, the more likely it is you'll get crucified too. His lessons, his teachings were valuable, not the fact that he was the lamb led to slaughter, which he never was. Jesus could and should have just gone into the hills and let his disciples carry on his teachings. They did anyway."

"So, are you are saying that Jesus is not a person to whom you can trust to keep you on the straight road?"

"I'd rather make the pact with myself or another being who at least came from my district, in a manner of speaking." "I believe, no one person can save another from themselves. It's got to be a mutual decision, one helping the other, someone who is tangibly there and who has the reality of the scene as it exists now. And it has to go both ways or it won't work."

"Well then, I'll make that pact with you on that basis, since I too by being a lay minister am trying to absolve myself—I'll correct that—balance the scales where I've done wrong things."

SECOND SÉANCE

C. Van Heyden

Over the intervening weeks, Elvis was on his guard. Catherine came by one night, she was a finalist in a local beauty pageant, but really insecure underneath the "beauty queen" façade.

"Elvis, why don't we get engaged?"

"Because, my love, we are not a match, we only dig some of the same things and that's not a reason to get engaged."

"All right, then let's pretend we are engaged, and I don't need a ring or anything."

Elvis could feel her intention though, and this time a cruel impulse rose in him, but like a balloon kept rising and went clear out of sight.

"I've got an idea, let's throw a party, and announce that we're going steady!"

"Steady?"

"Yeah, you know that's what girls call having one guy as a boyfriend they can count on."

"I like it. Can I invite anyone?"

"Sure, we have no secrets."

The observation Elvis most noticed about doing things on Earth, is that it is so easy to be distracted. Now, he simply wanted to stage a party to announce his going steady with Catherine, but as soon as he had begun promoting the idea he gets calls from seemingly out of nowhere, having nothing to do with the party. One of his old roommates calls him to ask for dough because he's moving to Florida, since his friend met a girl that lives there that he believes he'll marry eventually. Another "friend" from high school calls him up and tries to get him to join some real estate club to make money on the side. And another call from a PAC he never heard of, wanting donations to a campaign that isn't even going yet. Still, the party was a hit, everyone loved the fact that Catherine now had a steady boyfriend. Now, it was time to get back to Madame Chartreuse's séance.

When Madame C. next held a séance, it was in an abandoned warehouse. She said more room is often better for spirits to find us.

"So, I see most of us are again gathered together in hopes of reaching their loved ones departed or finding old friends from distant times."

At this séance there were a similar number of people, one man in a plug hat that looked like an undertaker, a couple couples, Matthew and his wife not amongst them, and various curiosity seekers we'd call them plus the token cynic.

The cynic spoke first, "Madame Chartreuse, is it possible that I could, that you could connect me with my deceased father?"

"What was your father's name?"

"Frank, but we, that is the family always called him by his middle name, Auggie. Short for Augustus."

"Come now into our midst, Auggie, your son is here and needs your presence to convince him of our authenticity."

Without histrionics of any kind a voice, male and low answered, "I am here son, but I am not able to see you."

"Dad, do you remember our dog?"

"Yes son, Rembrandt we called him and he died of a weak liver." This was correct in every detail. The skeptic though, did not show that he was emotionally troubled.

"But, what of it, are you testing the medium's abilities now?" This shocked the skeptic more than insulted him, but he proceeded as if he didn't hear this mild chastisement.

"I only wanted to be sure before I ask you this next question, which has been on my mind since you passed away in '94…in your will you stated that the inheritance from your estate should be divided equally amongst your brothers and all children, is that correct?"

"Yes", came the calm voice, as before. "All right then did you not mean when you stated, "all children" that my brother and I were included?"

"That was and is still my will."

"Then a grave injustice, I believe, has been wrought."
"Why?"

"Because the inheritance went to only your three brothers and their children, not to Cliff or myself! We were not included in the division."

"Then you are right, a grave injustice has occurred, because I loved you both, and I am sorry to know that you were left out."

"Dad, I am going to ask all those present here to bear witness of what has transpired, and although there is little legal chance of vindicating my brother and myself, I am comforted now that I was right in pressing for our share, and I will make a great effort to have your brothers attend a future séance and hear it with their own ears."

"As it should be, and I am willing to return as long as needed until this matter is rectified."

Having sensed the import and true purpose of his summoning, the voice of the called spirit ceased.

"Truly a marvelous interchange we have witnessed, and I am completely willing to affidavit what I have heard this day," promised Elvis. He then took control of the gathering's attention by asking Madame C. to once again call his brother in arms, Amtar.

"Amtar, please join us in this sacred gathering as you once before have done." This time there was no delay, and immediately Elvis was in touch with Joshua.

"My only question, Madame, is 'How were you able to get to Earth from Sellier?'"

This time there was another long silence. Elvis only prayed that Amtar now Joshua would not find himself barriered to this knowledge, as he himself was. Elvis hoped dearly that Joshua, not having nearly as rugged and checkered a history as himself would have much more clarity of memory.

"I cannot tell you that, yet I believe I should know it," came reply. At this, Elvis's heart sank deeply in his chest. If he was to ever get back to his home planet, at least the one he was ejected from on false criminal charges, he would have to find, discover, or build himself a method of returning and return, such is the nature of the native sense of justice so strong universally. Yet upon hearing Joshua's answer it became clear that the answer might never come.

Judging the distance to be in light-years, Elvis knew that conventional methods of space travel were centuries away from what he needed. Elvis began investigating teleportation. Nothing he read or saw on the Internet made much sense or seemed doable except that thought itself somehow could effect it. The only experiments capable of reproduction had to do with various transmissions of information, and small objects such as nails, matches and photographic paper, nothing that would work on a living organism. Then it hit him.

'I didn't come to Earth in a body form.' The other references available from the Internet were mainly biblical and Jewish mystical in nature, and so were talking about spiritual teleportation. But, however he got there Elvis wanted only to return to Sellier.

Elvis began cogitating on something that was very real to him. That dream or vision of him as a falcon. If he could get back his original powers, one of which was shape shifting, what then might he do to wend his way back to Sellier and away from this doomed life. He concluded that he somehow must increase his *philanthropic* contributions to society.

By now the idea of ever finding on Earth a reliable means of space navigation was dead. So, he knew the direction he had to go was in regaining his lost abilities. Somehow, Elvis knew, intuited that to just start shape-shifting without any real purpose wouldn't work. He knew from his studies of magic and sorcery that one didn't succeed with it on a whimsical basis. The power contained in this type of ability derives directly from the method and purpose of its use. He knew that well. 'What purpose could I find, that also would lend itself to exercising this shape-shifting ability?' This was his immediate problem then.

C. Van Heyden

EXILED TO EARTH

SHAPE SHIFTING

C. Van Heyden

The next day Elvis was reading in the campus weekly about a murder that was committed on campus and police were asking for information about it. 'This is where I could be of great help to the police' reflected Elvis. So, he traipsed down to the station to see what facts he could pick up.

A student had met his end in a shower. His name was Arthur, and he was a Sophomore. He had been shot once with a .45 in the chest. Police wanted anyone with data to come forth and make a report. Elvis decided to go undercover. That night he turned himself into a falcon and flew to the dormitory where the crime had occurred. He waited and watched for hours. Just watched. And around 2:00 AM a figure darted from behind a tree and made its way to the building he was watching. From the window Elvis could see the figure, a man not old, fairly tall with blond hair, wedging open the door with a small crowbar and entering. After a while the figure stooped and picked up something quite small and then departed. Seeing the sequence, Elvis concluded that the perpetrator of the killing returned to remove something that might incriminate him, so he followed the figure.

The man led him to a warehouse and a dimly lit room. Elvis flew straight in. There was another man waiting inside. The first man told the second, "I got the key." "Damn good that you did, and lucky nobody saw it and made an ID, or you would be in jail now." Then the two left the warehouse. The key had fingerprints, no doubt, but Elvis got a good look at the two men and could ID them to the police. What he would do is tell them that he was so horrified by the murder that he hung out last night just in case the suspect came again.

That's exactly what occurred the next day. The police were extremely pleased and cited Elvis as the hero. The police went directly to the warehouse found drugs and some notes and other evidence and fingerprints enough to convict the two men, who were, not surprisingly, drop outs from the college who had gone bad, and killed for drug money or the loss of it to Arthur. The upshot of this was now he had an in with the police department guys, and could probably utilize his powers of shape-shifting again and they wouldn't get too suspicious, now that he showed himself to be a concerned citizen and bold enough to do something about crime.

Now, Elvis thought, 'This is the time to get back with Joshua, let him know the scene, what he was doing, and tell him only enough to keep him interested in his efforts'.

...

When Joshua heard what Elvis had been doing, he got worried and cross with him.

"You shouldn't be putting yourself in dangerous positions Elvis, you know?"

"I never do."

"But tracking a killer, and a drug pusher...?"

"That was after the fact. You missed that I was concealed all the time, as I intended from the beginning; notice once they left the warehouse I didn't further track them."

"Something weird happened to me this week."
"What was it?"

During my sleep, or I might have only been day dreaming, but I swear a voice asked me about Sellier."

"What did you say?" "I didn't, I didn't have an answer. Isn't that strange?"

C. Van Heyden

"Were you trying to reach me?"

"Well I might have, I've been as you know talking about it, and I really do want to know how I got here from there. You've heard of clairaudience?

"No, never have, what is it?"

"It's the power to hear outside the usual distance of normal perception, a heightened sense of hearing, like the super sensitive smell of a basset hound only with hearing perception."

"And you believe I have that power?"

"I not only believe it, I know you have that power."

Let's try this, Joshua. Let me put you in a trance, a light trance and see if you have any submerged info about Sellier."

"I see, you're going to turn confessor to me, is that it?

"Let's try it and see what turns up."

All the time Elvis had been speaking to Joshua in a soothing tone of voice, now he continued this tone and increased it slightly and began swinging a silver chain to and fro in front of Joshua.

"I want you to just go into a day dreamy state here, not a deep trance…. Think of lying in a hammock in the shade on a perfectly clear cool day in summer with a soft breeze blowing gently across and around you…quietly, peacefully swaying…"

 Joshua's eyes close.
"You are under my direction…you are going back in time to when you left Sellier and nod your head when you arrive." Joshua nods.

"I'm asking you simple questions, and you'll give me the first answers that come to you…."

"What is your name?"

"Amtar"

What planet do you live on?"

"Sellier"

"What is your occupation?"

"Sculptor"

"Who are some of your friends?"

"Demetrius, Tallus, Nocturnis…"

"And your enemies?"

"Leebus, and Micah and his cronies."

"Tell me about the time just before you were sent to Earth."

"Police and spies and informers everywhere…I was accused of leading a revolt against The Almighty. Jesus had been crucified, his disciples imprisoned and anyone who had a following or formed opinion for the masses was suspect of disloyalty."

"What was your crime?"

"I lead the new school of thought called 'Institute of Practical Truths'."

"What was done to you?"

"I was declared 'incorrigible', my school shut down,

my students disbanded and threatened with deportation."

"What became of you?"

"…I was drugged, confined to a cylinder and shot into space."

"What system was used to launch?"

"Magnetic-gravitic."

"Could you replicate?" "No."

"When I next give a command, you will awaken fully and be under your own control, and I will no longer be directing your thoughts."

"Awake."

Joshua looked directly at Elvis, blinked twice, "That was terrific!"

"What was realest to you?"

"The loss of my school."

"So, it looks like I'm still stranded here on Earth." "Would you really go back if you could?"

"You bet I would, I've got nothing to hold me hear now; no romantic interests, no family to speak of, parents gone, my siblings far away and occupied with their lives...."

"I suppose it would be insane to tell anyone else what we now know?"

"Very, unless you enjoy being crucified."

"I suppose that it doesn't really matter that we know now what we know. It doesn't particularly elevate my ability to live my life, it's only fascinating and new, that's all, really...isn't it?"

"Right Joshua, so many people think knowledge is the huge weenie to go after, but knowledge without judgment is more likely to be a detriment."

"Amtar, hmm... there's something very satisfying though about just knowing that I have lived before. Granted it's a new look, but its importance fades in light of future prospects of living in a veritable hell for who knows how long."

"You know that's right, except for the few special times in my life when I was able to truly help someone, and a few accomplishments, life is mostly a drag most of the time."

"We spend most of our time trying to be good, instead of being what we want to be, regardless – just being, regardless of anything or anyone. The world must be full of lost souls who think they must do 'good' to get to someplace else instead of just going ahead and making this their *heaven*".

"I don't think I'm strong enough or smart enough, Elvis, to lead others to a better life, but I now know that a much better life is possible, that much I do know."

"And I must confess, Joshua, when I was an infant I knew that something quirky was going on…I knew right away somehow that I had…it's the déjà vu effect, you know?"

"I'm listening"

"One night I was so terrified, nearly berserk with terror, this horrendous nightmare of a sound and image kept repeating and repeating, like the 'Pit & The Pendulum'. This very loud rolling sound like a giant bowling ball was coming down on top of me getting louder and louder as it came on, and there was nothing I could do to stop it."

"What happened?"

'I went to my mother's bed, got in and still it wouldn't stop, and I cringed in the corner up against the wall and prayed for deliverance; and, still it kept on sounding, right in my mother's own bed. I tried to cover my ears but the sound wasn't coming from outside."

"How old were you?"

"Two."

"That's scary, very scary."

"I was sweating as if I had a 104 fever."

"And your mom?"

"I didn't wake her, I didn't want to wake her any more than when I got into the bed next to her, I just wanted to be near someone I could trust."

"Well if we can't tell anyone, then we should just go about our lives as if we didn't know."

"That's not going to work either, I'm sure of that. I'm going to keep on trying to find a way back to Sellier."

FORGING AHEAD

C. Van Heyden

.

Secretly, Joshua now had a hidden weapon with which to throw the religious scholars and academics who kept him boxed into thinking that the Bible was the word of God, and that heaven and hell were real places in some nebulous afterlife. Joshua's blood was at a boiling point, having bought into the fables as a child, and since, none of which ever did a damn thing for him when it counted.

In truth, he had taken the lay position hoping in some way he would have an experience or receive an inspiration that would confirm the beliefs he held that he accepted on faith. And no one ever told him about the Egyptian's concept of the soul and transmigration. They even knew less than what he knew now.

Ted Larkin was one of his school chums that was always giving him religious puzzles to figure out, and then laughing at him when his answer was wrong, according to Ted that is. The one Ted most liked to pull on Joshua was the one that went, "God can do anything can't he?" And Joshua would say "Yes, of course." Then Ted would smirk and say well can God make a stone so large that he can't move it?" And when Joshua answered either way, he'd come right back, "But you just said God could do anything!" Well now, Ted could ask that same asinine question and he'd be ready for him.

It made Joshua also curious about another belief he had bought into, predestination. Now that idea was shattered, and it made him wonder if he could still in his present life go back, or switch tracks and start successfully for a destination he had forsaken many years earlier. All his friends and their parents thought and told him that he'd make a good minister, in fact that they knew he was destined to be a minister. Just because he gave a fiery speech to the congregation at the age of twelve at his confirmation. He was neither pious nor reverent. But it seemed everyone else thought he was. So, it was when he told the then minister of his church that he was a conscientious objector to war, that made sense too, to everyone. But secretly he despised weaklings and people who tried to compromise with belligerents. If he had had a hero it would have had to have been George S. Patton, the general who manned the *Killer Battalion* in WWII.

What Joshua desired more than anything was to be martial arts master, like the samurai of legends he'd read about and fantasized. Joshua had been made to look the weakling in high school by a tough that was half his size, when he was trying to woo a cute saucy blonde a year his junior. Knowing that Marco had a gang, Joshua was humbled…but if knew jujitsu or karate he would have stood up for himself and not looked the fool in front of Gayle, and he detected that that is exactly what Gayle had wanted him to do.

On the other hand, Elvis was forging ahead in his quest to regain all his latent powers

...

By forging is meant, Elvis was going at it the only way he knew how. Get out and about and look for ways to use his "extra" powers profitably, that is, profitable for others.

"Catherine, what's happening with your Dad lately?"

"What do you mean?"

"Well, you told me he was about to get fired, right?"

"That's what he told me a few weeks ago, I merely passed it on to you."

"Well, did he get fired, what's the story?"
"Not that I know, he might not want to talk about it."

"Didn't you also tell me he's been beaten down pretty hard by a guy who is a V.P. in his department?"

"Yeah, a guy named Stockton." Dad has been fighting him forever it seems. Dad can draw circles around Stockton when it comes to car designs, and Stockton despises how good he is. But Stockton is also son of the owner so…"

I got an idea right then. Pay this guy a visit, turn on my clairaudience and pick up some dirt that dad can use to discredit him, since obviously he hasn't done so, so far, and the guy has to have done something bad for him to be down on dad so much. Probably embezzling tons of dough from his dad.

THE CAPER

C. Van Heyden

Paying Stockton *a visit* was the plan, but plans are just that, an intention to do something. MB Advanced Design Center isn't a place anyone can walk into for a tour, or is it? No, MB doesn't give daily tours, however after research it turns out that once a year the public can come to an open house and meet the designers and managers. Too long to wait, thought Elvis. I just need to get in the general vicinity of Stockton, and make sure when I go that he's not abroad or on vacation, and without letting Frank, her dad know I was there.

Next morning, Elvis entered the design studio with cell phone and Stockton's cell number purloined from Frank's phone that he let Catherine use when hers was in the shop. He called him to let him know there was a package from a local florist waiting for him that he had to sign for. When Stockton came out thinking it was a gag, he was taken aback by the beautiful bouquet, anonymously signed To: Stockton My boy! In the moments trailing, Elvis got a very good sounding behind the façade and what he heard was not pretty at all. In order to keep up appearances that he was a top designer himself, which he wasn't, he systematically had taken credit for a number of design innovations that he only approved. This to keep his father happy. This is why he was shocked to see the flower bouquet and the "My boy!" It pulled up the dirty deeds immediately and sub-vocally, but Elvis could hear them just as if he spoke them directly to the "delivery man". Stockton was getting very well paid for a job several others could do better than he, and he was taking credit where it was not earned, and he knew it. Frank was a target because somehow, sometime he did or said something that Stockton took as an accusation about just this enormous deception.

"Hey Catherine, do you know that I accidentally talked with Stockton yesterday by cell phone, and while I was talking to him, I got the distinct impression that he was hiding something, you know that hunted sound?"

"Not really, why did you call him?"

"Call it male intuition, but I think maybe Stockton is down on dad because dad may have discovered or may suspect Stockton of fleecing his own father, telling tall stories to him about his expertise, when in fact he's not half the designer dad is."

"But why did you call him?"

"It was an accident, a wrong number but he answered, 'Stockton here,'" so I said, "Excuse me, I made a bad dial, but did you say Stockton?" And he answered, "Yes."

"That's wild, my father-in-law Frank Bishop works in your office."

"That's right and only he has my cell phone number."

And I replied, "That's absolutely right and I'm using it now. He rented it out to his daughter my soon to be wife until hers comes back from the shop."

"And you got all that just from talking to him for a minute and a half?"

"Yeah, didn't you tell me Dad thinks he's a princox, and a know-it-all?"

"My dad thinks he's scared someone will take his job away who knows a lot more and can do a lot more."

"And he's right too. I'll bet if dad did a little survey—you know discreetly—he'd find out that Stockton has been puffing to his father these many years accomplishments in the design business that belong to dad and the other guys in his department.

Just to look good and keep the big bucks flowing in for practically nothing in exchange."

"But if my dad tried to embarrass Stockton, Stockton would get dad fired."

"Probably, unless your dad got him fired first. Catherine, why don't you invite your father over for dinner Friday night, and let's see if we can't do a little conspiring to get him out from under Stockton's thumb."

...

When Friday night arrived, Elvis had hatched a brilliant but simple plan, all he needed to do was convince Frank it was worth the risk.

"So, you're saying that I should feed Stockton a lousy design idea but make it look good on paper?"

"...that's the only way you'll get him off your back." You've been giving him the highest quality work for years and he's been giving you hell in return. He's probably doing something like signing his name to your work so as to look good to his father and stay on the payroll. Now it's time to give him something that justifies his ire."

"So, you're answer is to fight fire with fire?"

"In this case, I'm sure of it."

"But, how do you know that's the case?"

"Well, look at it. Is anything I'm saying sound real to you?" Look at how Stockton treated you the first year you worked for him, and compare it to lately, there was a change. That's why he's down on you and some of the other excellent designers in your group. He knows he's cheating you out of recognition, stealing it for his own personal benefit. And that in the eyes of his father would be enough to send him packing."

"The part about taking credit is true. He accepts awards as if they were his own, and hasn't given anyone in the department a raise since I've been there."

"No, he's mean-spirited that way. Let me level with you Frank, you know that cell phone you lent Catherine?"

"Yeah, what of it?"

"Well, she let me use it last week, and you know how if the lock isn't on accidentally you can dial a programmed number? That's what happened, and I got Stockton. In the process, I mentioned how I'd come to dial his number which is confidential, and he started talking about you."

"And what did he say?"

"Isn't what he said, but the manner in which he spoke. You see, I've observed that when a person talks critically of another with nothing good to say, then I begin to suspect that person's motives. He spoke as if he wanted to get something off his chest but all that came out was bad news about you. In fact he told me he was going to report you for breaking security by lending out your cell phone, to your daughter! That's mean-spirited."

"What you say may be true, but I'm not going to set him up for the fall. It'll come back to me and even if he does get removed, which is what I'm getting you think will happen, he'll can me before he goes."

"But you'll get hired back, after he's gone, that's the worst that can happen."

"No, I won't stoop to his type of game. Thanks."

"But dad, you told me you're likely to get fired any day now, so what's the difference?"

"The difference? I don't play dirty, and I'm not a quitter. I'd rather get fired, then Stockton can beat up on the rest of the guys until they quit, and then he will really get it from the old man, he might even disinherit him as well."

Elvis had to pay Frank respect, and let it go; not the result he was looking for at all. Catherine was equally disappointed.

C. Van Heyden

EXILED TO EARTH

VOLTE VIS

C. Van Heyden

Joshua was getting into trouble with his new found understanding of the cosmos. He was falling into that trap that most humans get into when they sense an upper hand. They wield it to their detriment over others, instead of using it to assist others.

Joshua was saying to Dennis, "What if you could determine without question that this life is not the only existence you have ever experienced? He wouldn't tell them anything about his stunning recall of Sellier, but he would keep at it until the target victim would just get exasperated and admit that it is possible. Only very few did admit it. Normally, it just provoked ridicule and anger.

"And so what, Josh, what if I did live before, I've got to deal with what's happening now. I've got enough problems, without looking for more."

"Right, but in the sense that you are free of the mystery surrounding life, doesn't that mean anything?"

"It means that this is the God awfullest place in Eternity."
"Precisely my point!"

"Unless we examine all the myths we've been fed about Heaven and Hell, God and the Devil, good people, bad people, oooh 'The Chosen People'. It's all a bunch of bunk, isn't it?"

"It makes me sick."

"Right, and add me to that."

"So what do you want me to do?"

"You've done it." "You've allowed yourself to not agree with the bunk. That's it, that's all."

"Something wants me to punch your face in Josh." "Yeah, I know, I got that urge too when it dawned on me."

"I've taken stock of my plans in life, and you know I think that what I'm doing is not really what I want to be doing. How's that for apples?"

"What are you saying?"

"That I'm not a minister, I'm not really interested in getting ordained or even finishing college."

"Whoa, that sounds like a big mistake."

"Ordinarily, it would be, but if a person knows that he'll live again, and I do, then success is a matter of setting a goal, no matter the difficulty, no matter the opposition, no matter the criticism, and seeing it through. That's what I'm talking about."

"What goal is that?"

"Ah, the million dollar question, Dennis, the million dollar question. Well, just now you'll forgive me for not disclosing all to your exalted self, newly of course. However, I will say that it is almost entirely a goal that is opposite to that of being a minister."

"Damn."

"Yeah, and luckily, I'm not too old to make it happen."

I wonder what my goal in life is, thought Dennis, and how did Josh come to be so sure of himself. At least, these were the type of questions, that probably Dennis was asking himself, as Joshua smugly but quietly walked away.

C. Van Heyden

CLARE

C. Van Heyden

Josh's mother was forever giving him the willies, always talking about divorcing dad, with no plans of what to do afterward, sometimes talking suicide. I put my attention there.

'This dame needs a shock or something to make her realize she is causing Josh a lot of grief, and herself the same' was my thought. Perhaps a visitation from a "messenger" would do the trick. Like the raven in Poe's story of the bereft student who sat lonesome amongst his books of forgotten lore trying to forget his deceased amour.

Or, I thought should I take the image of her deceased father who she strongly resembled and revered? Ah, this might be the stroke of a genius! If it failed however, it might shock her to death. But then even that would be better than the misery imposed upon her son.

When to enact such a device? Surely, not at nighttime, for that would be too startling and unsettling...it's supposed to be unsettling and startling.

How did she say her father spoke...laconically with a lilting almost breathless sweetness. So, I set about practicing.... That was the most difficult part. My voice was deep and sonorous, with no lilt whatsoever. Finally, I managed a semblance of a lilt.

Having never met her father or seen any photo, I elected to be his voice only; except that Joshua had told me once that his dad looked like the actor Bella Lugosi, quite the opposite image to his manner of speech—very dark eyebrows, dark eyes, facial hair and a rather compressed visage, like a face being squeezed between two powerful hands. I could manage that, I thought.

When the time arrived, I was unsure how I would open my conversation from the other side, and then it occurred to me. In the séance the dead were called into the presence of the living by a medium. But how would I get a medium to be in the same room with me, she didn't go to séances as far as I knew. But I did know a medium, and her voice, Madame Chartreuse! I telephoned Clare, Josh's mom and left a message, saying that I was in receipt of a "message" from her deceased father, and that the message said that he was trying to get in touch with her, but knew not where she was. So, I (the medium) located you and told him. Expect a visit any day from your deceased father.

Whether she listened to the message, or even

believed it if she did, I would pay her a visit, and set her straight on her behavior lately.

That night this is what happened: I left my body and appeared in the bedroom of Clare when she was reading. If she had been in the shower or on the toilet I would have left and reappeared at another time, but I timed it well. Although, now that I consider it, it may have been more impressive if I had appeared at one of those occasions.

"Clare, did you get the message from Madame Chartreuse? No reaction. "I told her to let you know that I needed to speak with you."

"Dad?"

"Do you not recognize my voice?"

"Am I dreaming?"

"No Clare, my darling, you are in your bed reading."

"But you are dead, aren't you?"

"In a manner of speaking, yes."

"Oh Daddy, I miss you terribly."

"I know. I have only a few words to say, and then I'll be gone."

"Where are you going?"

"It's not a place, but a state, Clare."

"But how can I reach you again?"

"You won't have to."

"You've been debating over leaving Fred and even thought of suicide."

At this Clare froze, and became pale.

"I can only counsel you as your father, Clare. I have always wanted you to be happy."

Clare began to weep.

"I'm not your father anymore, but I am conscious. And I am sure that you in my state would easily see where it is you have diverged from that happiness I wish for you." Keeping the lilt was getting harder and harder.

Clare stopped weeping.

Now I tried something I had never done before: I projected an image of Bella Lugosi into the space in front of Clare. But not too strongly.

She gasped.

"Clare, decide. Make a decision now. Create Fred as your husband, or divorce him."

Clare remained in a state of suspended motion.

"I'm going now, and won't be back ever again."

"NOooo! Don't leave." Clare reached for the image.

"Decide, Clare."

"Good bye, Clare."

And then I exited her bedroom.

C. Van Heyden

CRIMES WILL OUT

C. Van Heyden

It wasn't until a week more had passed when I got the news. I called Josh to tell him to set up another session. Josh told me, "Mom is divorcing dad."

"She's hired an attorney, filed the papers, and plans to move to New Jersey of all places. She says that's where she has always wanted to live."

"How does she look?"

"Different."

"Well, I'm glad for her because I for one was getting tired of hearing from you how bothered you were about it."

"So, you're glad for me too?"

"Naturally, you're my confessor, right?"

"More like I was your confessor, you've turned the tables on me to a large degree."

"No, I haven't I'm just following my destiny, besides two individuals don't have to be 'greater and lesser', as I think you discovered recently."

"I've discovered a lot of things recently, thanks to your persistence."

"Let's do another session, I've got some things to tell you."

"Where do you want to start back in?"

"Sellier. I reviewed in a session I was giving myself from notes, and I came across a piece of the missing puzzle."

"What was missing?"

"My attempt to overthrow The Almighty."

"Christmas!"

"Yeah that's what I thought."

"So, you were guilty of crimes?"

"Big time. In fact, I almost succeeded.

"Was I a part of it?"

"Yes, you were in on it too. You were intellectually challenging the hordes, while I was amassing an army of warriors who would take the capital, which was decaying rapidly, the heads of state that is and institute a type of benign martial law. Not like the Draconian martial law that's been so reactionary and common on

Earth after revolutions."

"And you remained undetected?"

"Not exactly. I was under surveillance as were most citizens at the time. And I was outspoken in dissent of The Almighty's declarations that were approaching Draconian Law, and made it known that I was against them."

"So, while I was trying peaceably to change the state of things, you were agitating for a real revolt?"

"That's what I found when I looked back over that time period, and the more I look back in short patches the more I see and the more I know what happened and why."

"So, accusation and the deportation were based upon a frame up because no one could prove you were agitating a revolt, just speaking freely about your disagreement, right?"

"Precisely."

"What did you do in reality?"

"I was getting to that. It seems whenever a country or

society begins to go to the dogs, it reaches a point where it targets and selects out the thinkers and doers and ascribes to them the most dastardly crimes and makes them public notice in the media in the most alarmingly lured but always grossly false details. It even sends out goon squads and starts riots in an effort to bring these thinkers and doers to an end. Then the decadent state thinks itself safe from further attack. It's an old hackneyed song worn out to the point of utter disgust. But still in vogue."

"And what did you do exactly?"

"I put together an elite band of counter vigilantes, pretty clever on my part, to dissuade the goons and hit men to think carefully of trying to force our best minds into asylums or outright kill them."

"For instance?"

"Oh, you want the gritty details, I see..."

"Well you know how ninjas quietly sneak up on their prey and knife them silently, well that was a specialty we had, and very effective. No licenses needed to buy or carry a sharp knife, no bullet shells to leave behind or gun to trace. Very, very clever and very daunting when the bodies start piling up three and four high as they did under my direction."

"How many did you kill?"

"I calculated about a hundred and forty over a period of a year."

"Did you regret any?"

"Odd you should ask that...there was one, I suppose in violence there is always collateral damage. This guy was a good friend of my sister. Named Colton and a good guy under normal circumstances. But he decided to be a mercenary when he got fired from his government post, and became a hired slayer. The sad part is he didn't really believe what he was doing was helping and that is what I'm sure brought his demise, and a rather cruel one."

"What did you do?"

"And I almost forgot to mention, we wore masks, something the goons didn't do, they were too arrogant to do that, "Working for The Almighty" was all they needed to know."

"So...?"

"I caught him one night trying to abduct my philosophy professor, and I shoved a dirk in his neck and watched him bleed to death."

"You say that as if you were cutting up some large steak in pieces to freeze."

"I'm disgusted with myself now, but not then. What was happening was too painful to let continue, and having the power to see and to be in places nobody expected, I could forestall many of the abductions and murders made to look like accidents."

"What was the effect on your sister?"

"Terrible. She went into shock for days and was ill."

"And the end?"

"There is no end to the killing until one realizes that it won't end by counter killing, which is what I realized. That is why I let myself be falsely accused and deported to Earth. It's all too simple now."

"Is that all you wanted to tell me?"

"No, I'm afraid the overall effect of my counter-vigilantes plan was to hasten the demise of any law and order, in other words it descended into a catastrophe much the way Rome descended into a licentious and decadent society and then expired with the exception of what was salvaged by the religious men of that age."

"Let's call it a day."

"Yes, let's do that, Josh"

C. Van Heyden

FINAL SÉANCE

C. Van Heyden

I didn't feel any return of other powers. It did however feel good to roll away a cloud of mystery that shrouded the causes of my debarment from my home planet.

But perhaps the most telling result of my confession is to realize that there probably isn't a planet worth going back to anyway. But I sure would like to have the freedom to know for certain about that.

And somewhere in all this I got this strange idea that there was some other place in the cosmos that was even more germane than Sellier, a place that I or anyone might truly think of as heaven. And this thought warmed me and pleased me to no end.

But if I couldn't get to Sellier, I certainly wouldn't be able to contrive getting to a more distant or older world. Thus, I turned my thoughts again to Madame Chartreuse. If Josh and I had come from the same planet to Earth, why not others?

"Madame C, can you arrange a session with just your most devoted followers?"

"I believe I could, and for what time period were you thinking?"

"Next Friday night?"

"That might be a little too soon, but I gather that you have a pressing need, so I'll give it my utmost attention."

"That's exactly my thoughts."

The night arrived with more than twenty in attendance. One person said they could only stay a short time, but was there to see what all the excitement was about. These types usually just obfuscated the séance with silly questions and "plausible" explanations for anything supernal that occurred.

"Madame Chartreuse would you ask that all in attendance put their attention on 'Those from the world of Sellier'?

"We who are gathered here in the quest for truth, pay heed to those whose lineage stems directly or indirectly from 'Sellier' a planet in the cosmos."

All nodded in agreement, but again the wait was very long. During which time there was much murmuring and musing.

What worried me at first is that Josh would also turn up, and probably be the only one. Then, they started coming in droves. And most were not happy to be summoned.

"Why do you wake us?"

"A man amongst us here is pining to go back to Sellier, he is adrift on Earth and wishes to find companions that can assist him in returning."

There was a tumult of voices so that nothing could be understood. Then when that quieted down, I asked Madame C. to mention the name 'The Almighty'. She did and then two voices wrung out clearly.

"The Almighty was once a great man, a great leader. But he was suborned by men who envied his power."
I asked Madame C. to ask if they were here living on Earth, and they said no, that they were still in limbo and disenfranchised.

I was tentative but I directed her to inquire as to how they were debarred from normal existence.

"We were summoned, accused, condemned and then thrust into space as punishment. The canister ship was detonated and we are now suspended in the ether."

I could see that these utterly lost souls would be of no use to me.

It was time to break away from this madness. There was too much debris on Earth. The more beings in a given area the more debris. The more debris, the more madness.

I decided to go on a tour of the States. I had saved money from the previous summer job, and in late May after finals I began.

...

Washington D.C. was the first stop. As a child I'd seen the Liberty Bell and Valley Forge, but I'd never been to the Capitol of the country I lived in. When I got there, I was surprised to find that it wasn't a crime ridden, slum infested city whose image somehow had grown up in my mind for "D.C." Probably had it mixed in with "Detroit".

People were not particularly warm, but everyone seemed to have a purpose and a destination, streets were clean, the air was clean...I found out that large trucks were forbidden inside the city limits.

Strangely or not strangely then, capitols are about the same everywhere, even on distant planets. In order to preserve the image of imperturbability / immutability everything is built of stone. Always imposing, always...containing the basic geometric shapes, cylinder, pyramid, rectangle. I observed there is a tremendous amount of order in the universe, not so in person's lives. If I did wind up forever stranded on Earth, then I'd better plan to straighten things out here, no matter the size of the task. That's what Man has been trying to do with his "civilizations" all along hasn't he?

My next stop was Texas. All my life I had heard how it was the great state, so vast and untamable by mere men.

But Texas as with the other states had succumbed to civilization and industrialization. Still it was away from home and there seemed to be more room for everyone. Dallas, Austin, San Antonio not to mention Laredo all still had a frontier aspect to them, whereas Los Angeles, New York, San Francisco never had a frontier feel.

In New Orleans I ran across a steak house that only served steak, just steak, no potatoes no salad, not anything else, sort of the beef-eaters version of a Roscoe's Chicken Emporium only minus the fixings.

Now, readers may be wondering whether or not I

was traveling to these various places in the shape of a falcon or another flying creature...well no, I decided I couldn't really experience a get-away if I were destined to return to my point of origin, and again I couldn't use that power really unless the occasion called for it in some profound and necessary way. Plus, I couldn't ride the old trolleys that way and get much out of it or sample the great variety of gumbo that permeates the city's restaurants and is all encompassing as a menu item in the city that has its own style of jazz.

I must say though that the Cajun shrimp was a little too spicy or dicey, because by night end I had a flaming stomach ache that wouldn't quit. And as for the summer heat, well only if I could have turned myself into an alligator would I have even vaguely approached any relief from the super humidity – humidity by the way that the indigenous habitants seemed perfectly accustomed to and seemed further to enjoy wearing suits and ties on days when I would have had on a thong. The crime rate was high, but no one bothered me, and I didn't see any evidences of violence. What I did see, and feel was a beautiful but somewhat melancholy spirit that filled the entire city and in some ways was its protector. Unmistakable.

Next was San Francisco...and if ever there was a city to pine over, if you can't live there or go there at will, this is that city. Somewhere in Greece, ancient Greece there was a city like this in character, and here in modern times minus or should I say with other superstitions replacing those that Greeks possessed stands a monument to a civilization that neither knows how great it could be nor how far it has fallen from the ideal.

Blue skies most of the time; great vistas of the stormy ocean from Knob Hill, tall buildings and mansions like New York City but not so tall as to be overwhelming sometimes; and just the dearest, quaintest most reliable and downright useful trolley system, I think, in the world.

While I was in S.F. at the airport I met a girl, who seemed to be saying with her eyes let's get together. Shortly thereafter I found myself in a co-ed bathroom undoing her summer blouse. This isn't a confession, merely an interesting occurrence in that city. And another time I was ringing doorbells to find exact directions in a neighborhood and a lovely lass invited me in, in her bathrobe. After a few minutes it was clear to me that she was considering ménage a two, but I had to get to my next destination and dallying in someone else's home could lead to unhappy consequences.

C. Van Heyden

The time spent in Portland Oregon was amongst the best of all places I visited. In May, spring is in full swing and the city famous for its roses and rose festival is gorgeous. Edifices all proportioned, none too tall or too squat, clean streets and no graffiti. People mostly going about daily routines but willing to talk with a stranger.

One night in June I went for a walk and for the first time I witnessed the Aurora Borealis, "Northern Lights", easily one of the best natural phenomena that nature has to offer Man. As surprising, the daylight hadn't begun to fade until nearly 10PM. That gave me also for the first time the idea of what it must be like living above the arctic circle where days last sometimes eighteen hours or more.

Of course, there was rain—lots of it—but how else could flowers thrive in Portland.

North Carolina, Durham area and Chapel Hill–now there's a location I could really say is sweet—near the ocean, lots of pretty scenery, the best damn crab salad anywhere—healthy large portions and cheap too!

This getaway was wondrous for my morale. I became charitable. I pulled myself away from the big cities for the small towns and it worked.

I had heard that Niagara Falls was a great place to visit, and I found it so. However, the town of Buffalo nearby was by comparison a grotesque death trap where the coal fumes from manufacturers pitted car finishes inside two years, and the winter doing more damage underneath, not to mention damage to human lungs from the soot and fumes constantly raining down, and afloat in the air.

One very unusual occurrence happened in Buffalo.

It began raining one morning and being out in it without umbrella I sought shelter. I see a set of very tall ornate doors. I proceed to them and to test them for admittance. Surprisingly they open with ease. I enter. I am in the vestibule of a cathedral. No one is present, I hear only the air I'm breathing passing in and out of my body. My thoughts, 'well no one is here and I'm not intruding on a church service, neither do I mean any harm, aren't churches the last refuge for the weary or downtrodden'? Taking up a seat in a varnished pew near the entrance I take in and enjoy as I can the quietude, and it is beginning to help me relax. I wonder should I pray…now would be a good time as any, since I do not know what my future will be should I never find an egress to Sellier.

I have no ken with nor any patriotic spirit for America or for that matter this Earth. I am sitting alone and quiet, even pious. Suddenly, a thundering chord announces the beginning of an organ recital in the cathedral and proceeds to another and another – and then a quickened and very rapid escalation of notes and I am frozen in disbelief but crazy mysterious joy at what I am hearing. I can see no one, I cannot even see the organ or from where the masterful sounds are coming. I get up and walk to the aisle and peer up at where organs I know sit above naves. But no organ can I see, yet I hear it and it is Bach. I know the sound of Bach and it is a Fugue! I know it. Back down I sit. I'm enraptured – yes. Yes, that is what I feel now. The music, Bach is speaking to me, is enfolding me in his loving arms with this incredible fugue. I am blessed. I am alive!

I listen very carefully to all the notes, every note. This is happening! Is the organ playing by the hand of God --when will he reveal himself...or has he already? Who is the organist?? Why do I not hear his feet upon the pedals? Will I know when it is finally over? I am expectant. The fugue ends. There is no applause. Bach is no more, the church is quiet again, very quiet. I start to open my mouth to say, who are you, where are you, how did you know I was here, how did you know I desperately needed this? Childishly I believe it would undo everything now to hear an answer. I wait for a door to open, for the sound of a footstep to give it all away, to break the spell, the enchantment. I hear nothing. I see nothing moving. The experience is complete. The moment is over.

It is still raining when I exit.

At no time did I even have the inclination to invoke any shape changing powers or any extended auditory powers, I was simply a typical terrestrial tourist visiting places "on vacation".

I just have to add this part about a woman who spent all her days every day all day cleaning her house. Why? Because she had two boys die from skin poisoning, and she wasn't about to let her third and last child die that way. Her name was Eloise, and she wouldn't let her son have any colored socks because the sweat might make the dye in them run and get into his bloodstream and kill him too. And, I imagine although I never heard her say it but, all his pants and shirts had to be colorfast and preshrunk or she wouldn't buy them for him to wear. And cleaning her house so that it was immaculate was her way of fighting off the evil thing that had taken her first two sons. But, otherwise she was a nice person. Yet oh, the waste of a lifetime...she could have taken just two hours a day and learned a new language, or read a book that would give her some insight to other peoples and other places. Who knows that she couldn't have gotten herself educated this way, many have, and been much more supportive of herself and her remaining son, but she chose to live on welfare and insist on a perfectly clean house.

Getting back to California and the "big cities" was a minor shock for me, I have always liked the variety available in big cities – the chance to meet foreigners, sample food other than American, read exotic books and such and visit many and interesting places, the likes of which small towns run out of quickly.

I must confess after all the traveling I should have written a travelogue and published it. What I did do was start writing a book about the kinds of people I met in various places and what some of them got me to thinking about. Like, this issue with pro-rights and anti-abortion. Why focus on the solution or no solution to a problem that shouldn't exist in the first place? Who in their right mind would object to a woman aborting a child if the child is deformed to the point where one and all know it will be a burden to itself, the family, and community? Or for that matter on the mother's life, albeit this instance is very rare, these days. Focus on educating the woman. Focus on that. I see it this way. Women want to have children, and it's a good thing, and the sexual act is how it's done. And it's natural to want to have sex and the pleasure it brings, or supposed to bring. So, focus on those things, but also make other details known and well thought of and drop all the added unnecessary prohibitions and warnings. Young females know their own sexual function. What they don't know is the whole story of birth and raising a child. Teach that, teach all of it. Teach it with dignity and with sobriety. Have small groups of teenage girls sit and watch a woman give birth in a hospital, an easy delivery. Done in person or on closed circuit TV. Then one that is not an easy delivery. With that knowledge watch the number of abortions drop like a boulder off El Capitan.

Earthlings are sometimes just too goofy.

Then there was this guy who snored loudly – VERY LOUDLY, that I had to share a room with because we both got to the hotel at the same time and it was what... 1:00 AM and I and he were dog tired. So, we agreed to share the only available accommodations, or have to sleep in our cars. Well that's what I wound up doing, after trying the bath tub with the door shut. Man, this guy could put a lighthouse foghorn to shame. I asked for a rebate on half the night, but that didn't work either. Then it hit me. There are probably a large number of persons who can't sleep a good night's sleep, but it's so easy once you realize one thing. That the body needs its rest but that we don't, particularly. That's why it's always a good policy to keep one's activities organized. Try not to let commotion stay unhandled by days end. Keep things tidy that way, then there's only the body's issues to handle. That can be best handled, if needed by a long walk or sometimes I'll take 'er out for a two mile sprint and tire the livin' ?$&@ out of it.

Well, I'm feeling all oriented again so back to my other confessions.

When I got back to Layton, Joshua was nowhere to be found. I had emailed him before turning around on my tour of America to head home. So, I went researching around campus.

I checked with some of Joshua's frat brothers, nothing. No notes either.

MASTER CHIP TY DICK

C. Van Heyden

Joshua had taken off for China, seems he really meant it when he told me martial arts master was his true goal.

I received an overseas call around a month after I got home again, and it was Josh telling me how exciting it was to be in Fengcheng four hundred miles south of Peking, a village of no import but the home of an old Taekwondo master. He was studying with him, even though the master had not for a long time taught pupils. Josh had alluded to a "dream" that was so vivid instructing him to follow his heart, that the old master recanted and reluctantly accepted him.

Then I got another call about two weeks later:

"It will take a year to two before I'm allowed to study the advanced arts of Tae, but it is going to be well worth it. This old master is the guy who taught some of the world's best in the last half century. Meanwhile he's got me making and piling bricks for his new house."

"How did Clare take the news that you were leaving for the Orient?"

"Oh, amazingly calm. She even chipped in a few hundred bucks for my travel expenses."

'Wow', thought Elvis, 'I really did have an effect on her.' "You know, after confessing all those 'things' I had done in China, I feel like I could visit again, and maybe even visit you."

"Now, that would be an awesome surprise."

"Say Elvis, you want to know something freakish?"

"What's that?"

"This master, his name is Chip Ty Dick, first off, which I think is a great name, and I think he might even listen if I told him about how really I came to decide on martial arts."

"You're right, the orient has been a bastion for centuries of the spiritual masters. Look at Thailand almost one hundred percent Buddhists in that country, and they like the American Indians did for a long time positively know that they have lived previous existences."

"That's what I'm saying, this guy first of all to do the feats he's capable of must know that he is more than just a pile of muscles and bones...I kind of wonder that he probably also knows I was hedging about the "dream" but took it anyway, knowing what he does as master."

"So, tell me more about this Master Dick."

"He's a funny guy, he likes to pull tricks on me."

"As in?"

"He says try walking around the pile of bricks while placing them down, so as to get better distribution. Twice I've fallen over, because it is impossible to do so without losing balance. He's is teaching me Tae by making me see its basic elements."

"That is funny."

"He also splashes me with cold water now and then while I'm sleeping to see if I'll react with anger or not." He says, one must never react to any situation, only respond as the situation dictates. The roof may have given way and splashed you with water, are you going to solve it by getting angry at the roof?"

"What else can you tell me about him?"

"Well, I'm not sure, but I think he's a coyote part time."

"Tell me more about that."

"Well, a coyote or...fox may be a better way to describe what I've seen."

"Tell me, what have you seen?"

"Master Dick tells me he needs to go into town for provisions, but he leaves in the late afternoon – then later I spy this fox up on a hill overlooking where I am, as if he's watching or keeping watch on me."

"Go on..."

"Master Dick does not return until the next morning. And he isn't carrying any victuals. I once asked him if he stayed over in the village and he says, what I do is not your business to know when I am gone from home."

At this point, I think 'This master is a shape changer too', and who knows what else. And now I want to meet and talk with him. As Josh says he must know quite a lot about the spirit side of life, if he is as capable as his reputation states.

EXILED TO EARTH

FENGCHENG – CHINA

C. Van Heyden

I had not been to the orient in this lifetime, and so I didn't have any preconceived ideas or already formulated ones about China, India, Japan etc. What I found truly I must confess startled my conscience in no small way.

As with any civilization that has lasted the millenniums, China was a spiritual nation of great proportions. But a spirit can be alive to a great degree or it can be nearly dead and trying to awaken again. China, I found was in the latter state. There is to the eye unsurpassed ancient beauty there, and concurrently there are also many vestiges of brutal despair. I perceived in Peking much of the brutal despair, and in the village of Fengcheng much more of the former. I gathered that where great masses of humans congregate there also amasses the influence that makes by numbers alone an inhuman atmosphere where identity is lost but replaced with a non-entity. The same perception which earlier was the cause of leaving Layton for an elongated sojourn away from the big cities.

Master Dick met me at the gateway to his house. I saw the new house behind in its incipient stage, but I did not see how he knew that I was approaching his home, since I gave no notice of when I would arrive, and there are hedges higher than that of a tall man surrounding his camp. He grabbed my hand offered firmly and with a genuine smile invited me to his domicile. Josh was in the field behind working as usual on making bricks and such. I assumed correctly that Josh had foretold him of my desire to visit. It's a truism that oriental philosophies and ways of living are all based upon the idea of limitless time, there never is a hurry and to hurry is in itself a discreditable act and can bring dishonor to the one insisting on haste.

The house, though destined by its layout to be much larger in capacity than the rustic home of the master, was even after several months only a shadow of what it would become when finished. I was reminded of a story about haste, while I surveyed the grounds: a traveling old man and his burrow were overtaken on a high hill road by a troupe of similar travelers that at once told the old man that he should speed up so as to get to the town just over the next rise where he could rest and enjoy the fruits of the civilized townspeople. The old man curbed his animal so that the eager intrepids could pass and be gone on their way, saying to them, "I am in no hurry." Much later, still not near the forecasted town, the old man heard a thundering sound the likes of which he had never heard before and a flash of light more brilliant than the sun. When at last he gained the rise and looked down he saw only a burnt out (radioactive) city.

After entering, I was immediately taken by the exquisite, completely aesthetic furnishings and art that adorned the interior, and were the antithesis of the exterior of his rural cabin. He had on his main wall a gigantic painting of a lush forest landscape with two pagodas in the distance but distinctly portrayed. Covering his floor was a large woven carpet of surpassing beauty, and I wondered how he was able to keep it so cleanly brilliant, especially when I learned it was handed down to him by his father as a bridal gift many years ago.

This was no hermit lodge either, for he had stocked his kitchen with a robust blender and all the usual accoutrements of a modern kitchen. Parked in the very rear was a fancy Jacuzzi as well. However, the unit was self-sufficient running on two generators, one back-up that could run on propane as well as diesel. In a word this rustic lodge was Master Dick's fortress.

"Call me Chip", sighed the Master as I told him of my plane flight into the mainland from Heathrow airport. This I took as a very good sign, and rightly so. Later I noticed Josh never deviated from addressing him as Master...no other title or affectation added.

"Thank you, Josh told me that he is deeply indebted and appreciates your most gracious offer to take him as a pupil."

"I did so, only because, I perceived a righteousness in the request, which I admit many times before I did not look for in previous supplicant's determination."

"I would like to take Josh to dinner in town, if that is all right?"

"No, it is not all right. His stay here is indefinite and until he reaches maturity as a graduate. I will not allow his training in any way to be incurred by outside agitation or influence of any kind. We eat together, a measured diet and scrupulously so as to afford ourselves the very best vantage mentally and physically for understanding marital arts and their purposes."

"Then I presume that I am not welcome?"

"What foolishness to ask that. You are welcome, or I would not have let you come inside the gates."

Master Dick's response was not heated or defensive in any way, it was done with superb control of his faculties and I understood it at once.

"Well then, I am also grateful and honored to be so welcome."

"You shall stay in town but when you are here you are my guest, and dinner is precisely at 7PM, and it is one hour 'til then."

....

Master Dick, as I will refer to him in this confession, is a man of slight figure, no more than five feet four or five feet five inches tall and weighing I estimate about 120 to 130 pounds. But in the orient this is usual, and as for martial arts, well that's what chi is for—using the force of your opponent at every opportunity and thrusting with the rotating movement of the whole body while pushing down as gravity would do no matter the skill, giving the most powerful stance and adding immeasurably to the unity of the Tae or the Kwon. At somewhere around seventy-five years he had yet to develop any appreciable gray, nor did he have any deep wrinkles, only the ones at the outside corners of each of his eyes that were to all appearances makeup.

Master Dick, a consummate chef, prepared a sumptuous dish of fragrant seaweed, thinly sliced and lightly broiled pomfret in peanut oil with a salad garnish including bits of artichoke, bok choy, bean sprouts sliced peppers and water chestnuts. A meal after which I perceived the room and the scents coming from the kitchen with clarity as though I had been given a perception intensifier to wear.

Josh started off the conversation with a mundane fact: "I've got nearly enough bricks made for the entire south wall, Master."

"Fine, and you made sure that they are all of the same exact size?"

"Whoa, that is something I haven't been doing."

"My instructions were to take the test brick that is marked clearly on the bottom as TEST and for each brick made compare and see that they match."

"I apologize, Master."

"No apologies needed, just do it right. And have you checked each one for not too deep a frog?"

"Yes, I have been eyeing each one on that count."

"Good, then all is in order so long as the dimensions are kept standard and we can proceed with the first wall as soon as we have attained enough of them."

At that Master Dick motioned with his head that it would be time for my departure adding in a soft voice that Josh must be asleep for rest by 8:30 PM so as to be ready to work at 4:30AM as the sun rises the next day. I bid Master Dick a fond goodbye and asked when I could visit again, so as to have some time to talk with Josh about personal matters.

"You are welcome to come back on Saturday, when he has his personal time allotted, in the afternoon when it will be to your advantage."

As I left, I too began to wonder how intuitive Master Dick may truly be, as Josh had hinted in his first phone call.

C. Van Heyden

EXILED TO EARTH

AWAITING A SIGN

C. Van Heyden

In the town of Fengcheng there is a hotel with a balcony. I took a room upstairs and proceeded to plan my approach to finding out if Master Dick could afford any knowledge to me for returning to Sellier.

When I told Josh I would visit, I cautioned him to not do any preliminary foraging for data from Master Dick, and this was good advice since Master Dick with his high degree of perception would have deciphered Josh's intent and dismissed him.

Why didn't I just come clean and ask for the information I wanted? I was there to visit Josh as well as revisit a land I once called home, and if lucky might also derive vital information I personally needed to make my way back to my older homeland. And as mentioned earlier, any inclination towards hurry would be sorely taken and would cast suspicions on Josh's presence altogether. Neither of which are productive.

If I had only known before I left on my tour of America, I would have forfeited that effort and made my way to the Orient, because here was true peace and tranquility in a style that was timeless and beautiful beyond reason.

There was a bookstore around the block from the

hotel, and I sought texts on Taekwondo and any Chinese mysticism or mythology. One such volume contained the stories from ancient times when spirits and immortals mixed company with human heroes. None mentioned beings from other places in the Universe, only the typical stories of lust and betrayal and wars for territorial domination and revenge. And then it occurred to me...when Master Dick goes out of his camp and doesn't return 'til next day, I will try to find him in whatever form he takes and as a falcon I will find him and communicate with him. This was the plan.

....

When I awoke at daybreak, I realized first that Josh was already up and going through or finished his basic martial art exercises. The townspeople were yet to stir though I did smell something pungent wafting through my patio doors which told me someone was in the kitchen of the hotel working on breakfast. There was jasmine tea, jasmine rice in a bowl steaming and an assortment of egg dishes waiting for me when I made my way into the dining area. A few locals were already sipping tea and talking amiably. No one looked up or in my direction. I sought the manager's attention who spoke English clearly but slowly, to tell him that I might be staying a number of days and I wanted a lower rate for the duration. He understood and said he would consult the owner if I were to tell him a specific time they could have me as a guest. My answer was at least one month. This cheered the manager. I sat down and enjoyed another oriental style meal in a land I was growing fonder of by the minute.

I was leafing through the book on Chinese mythology and came across a reference. It reminded me of another similar story in a book published in America about the supernatural, and that one spoke of how real records of visitations to Earth from aliens could be found as far back as the 13th century, with illuminated plates from those records. The pictures as I was reminded of them consisted of oblong space craft not drawn at all to proportion but just depicted up in the air above the heads of persons looking up or going about their daily business. You would think such a shocking altogether unusual occurrence would give cause to someone with decent drawing skills to get a much better rendition of what they saw flying around in the sky when no other such object except birds or a cannonball in that time were known to fly through the air. So, I thought at the time it was drawn by someone who was told it was so, not by a person who was there when it happened.

All the stories in the mythology, like those I had read when I was in high school were from times long, long ago. 'Isn't it amazing' I pondered, 'that stories which are obviously incredible could come down through the ages and still be read by many, when no one would credit them with anything remotely resembling truth, these days.'

The manager came to my room with good news, the owner would be happy to offer a twenty percent discount for a stay of one month or longer. I thanked and tipped him. Since Master Dick was only known to "go into town" or disappear in the late afternoon, I waited and read more stories, while drinking more white tea.

I found nothing to correct about Fengcheng or the people or their culture, just the opposite of my defacto home in the states.

One might conclude that in order to have a non-militant society and yet safe from most oppression, martial arts would have to be the only answer on a personal level. True, tanks are hard to defeat with Taekwondo or any martial art, but holding a "conquered society" is going to be extremely daunting if each individual in the society is capable of taking on several adversaries and whipping them with their own force. That would keep me sleeping and living in a peaceful state of mind, and giving would-be tyrants much to consider before they vent their agitated troubles upon fellow inhabitants. And if each individual was also aware of their true immortality, as

Buddhists are, there could be no lasting subjugation. Even the divinities of the ancient myths knew when they offended too much they soon lost their powers and freedom.

I didn't expect to hear from Josh while I was in town, unless it was to alert me to the departure of Master Dick, so any phone call only meant that. Two days and nights passed before a call from Josh. He was excited to tell me that Master Dick foretold him of his leaving the next day for town and that he wouldn't be back until the next day. But this coincided with the Master's usual trip once a month for real to get various necessities. So, I was not sure if this meant it was time to seek Master Dick in his other forms. I could certainly go out on a scout, no harm to that. At no time when I was in Master Dick's company was I able to detect any of his thoughts at variance with what he said to me, which further corroborated his status of Master.

This time I confess I was not so sure of the rightness of what I was planning. And then again, I had little choice. But I resolved not to confront Master Dick if I should come upon him in altered form, since that would be a mistake in terms of Josh's status and safety at the camp. I would however observe the observer to see what if anything I could do to broach the subject to

Master Dick next time I visited his home. As this turned out, it was the weakest solution.

EXILED TO EARTH

STILL IN EXILE

C. Van Heyden

As I soared over the terraced hill adjacent to Master Dick's camp, I noticed a furry animal beside a large tree looking in the direction of where Josh was working. Almost at once it looked at me (falcon) and began to study. Whether fox, or wolverine or wolf, it didn't matter since instinctively I would not attack it unless it was encroaching on my nest. Nonetheless it became wary of my presence and stopped looking towards Josh. I did perceive an uneasiness and a definite dislike for intruding on its space. I flew away from the hill, but after kept an eye on the form for a while.

Contemplating my next move back at the hotel, I got the notion that I should just wait for Josh to complete his studies with Master Dick, graduate and then entirely separate from that whole affair approach the Master about my needs. I could stay for several months in China, what with the cost of living about one sixth of that back home. I feared I may have already cast doubt on my presence with Master Dick, and was uneasy thinking of going back to visit Josh under some pretext.

It must be difficult for those who remain cut off from other life forms because they believe they can't communicate with them. We love our pets and believe that we can influence them and maybe occasionally train them, but for most the idea of talking with a leopard, a horse, a cow, a cricket just seems beyond possibility, when in fact it is not only possible it is easy, if one gets the idea first that it can be done and is not unnatural. We hear of horse whisperers, and we love the cartoons where animals are discussing human behavior and think that is okay. Aren't these life forms that can receive a thought? They surely communicate amongst themselves even if it is only in a stampede of cattle or zebras running from a lion. As long as the shape and look of the shell are different the being using it thinks all too often, I can't be real to that other being who is using a dissimilar shell for its home base. Yet there are even mythological stories of wolves suckling human babies, and these stories have survived the millennia.

I was just as concerned about Josh achieving his goal with Master Dick as I was in plumbing Master Dick's intellect and abilities. I conveyed my disappointment in trying to intercept Master Dick on the hill, to Josh, but he already knew. Master Dick had mentioned in passing something about the aborted meeting indirectly the next day, and Josh knew that his master had suspected someone was watching him.

The first south facing wall was ready for assembly now that enough bricks and mortar were made available through Josh's efforts. So began that phase of Josh's apprenticeship. I chose to go in search of more data about the Chinese province Fengshan, of which Fengcheng was a town.

My impulse was to buy a backpack and go into the mountains. There I would seek to connect with any other mystical or martial arts figures. So I decided to take a holiday away from the town, away from any temptation to prematurely confront Master Dick. With the manager's permission I subleased my hotel room for two weeks and began my journey. I had no idea, but soon realized the mountains around Fengsheng were unusually shaped but far from considerable in height. I wondered if I would find any men there that shared any skills that matched my own.

....

While I was gone I found that Josh confessed to his Master that he had revealed information about Master Dick's coming and going to me, and his master was not pleased. But for myself I wanted to climb for the exercise, get above the city for a view, while searching for a man, someone, anyone like Chip Ty Dick.

In the two weeks that I was traipsing the hills, no other martial arts or Chinese gurus came across my path as I wandered. I reluctantly concluded that I would return home, and try my luck there, and have the advantage of speaking to prospects in English. I telephoned Joshua from the hotel that I was leaving the next day. Josh was saddened, mainly because he had come to the realization that he felt more suited to this type of life than to the university life, and that we would probably not see each other again. I paid the hotel manager the difference, since I reneged on the monthly agreement, leaving more than enough money to get a plane back to the states.

I also resolved to not give up.

Ever.

Faithfully, James (Friend of the alien)

PART II

FOX AND FALCON

BACK IN LAYTON

C. Van Heyden

"You know who Seymour Traher was? Not likely," Elvis spoke out loud to no one in particular. 'He was the first and only man who told me, *Life is great, if you just don't weaken*.' Elvis reflected as the plane flight wearied him into daydreaming.

'He was a book salesman. He also smuggled exotic birds into the U.S. and I surmise that may have been his primary source of income. If I hadn't dodged the draft, moved from New York to California, and under an assumed name sold encyclopedias I never would have met Seymour.' And he drifted off further.

Getting back home from China for Elvis was easy by jet plane, the contrast in civilization was not easy. He had lost his close friend and confidant to the much more civil world of Fengcheng, the small village where Joshua would eventually attain Martial Arts Master. All he had to look forward to was more searching, and to tell his findings or experiences, perhaps even his success, but no one to tell them to, he thought.

He told me (James), "No doubt my help to the local police was still something I could fall back on, but Layton, although close to the big cities, was a sleepy town in the main, nothing very news worthy happened, being a small college community. My thoughts turned now to Catherine and her father Frank, but mainly C. Could it be that I was destined to marry this filly. If I did, how could I ever then leave Earth?"

Catherine had evolved to a much more tolerant person since our going steady party. My affinity for her increased even when I sojourned in places far from Layton. We had stayed in touch by telephone and when I returned we consummated our desires in a week-long tryst of pure love-making that would have made a bacchanal blush.

I discovered that Josh had given all of his notes of our sessions to you to compile. Of course, I presumed you would keep them confidential and sacrosanct.

Frank had somehow avoided confrontation with Stockton and was still working at MB Advanced Design Center, and as far as Catherine could tell not slated to be fired.

I stopped by the sheriff's office just to let him know that I would be available. Sheriff Bradford told me things were quiet since that college drug related murder incident. That's how he referred to it. I felt compressed. Most of my savings were gone, the largest part used up for my excursion to China, and before that my expedition around the U.S. to find solace and perhaps a kindred spirit who could assist my efforts to get back to Sellier.

"Catherine, when I was away did anyone call for me?"

"Not that I remember, but I was not home all day each day either."

So far, I had not told Catherine about my powers, but it seemed that it was not possible to keep the secret from her.

My third year at Bingham University was soon to start, my days would now be entirely filled up with class work, homework, research and perhaps a football game now and then. Oh, and church. Turning twenty was nothing, in the manner of Mark Twain, "I've done it a thousand times."

What I needed to do *a thousand times* more were acts calculated to raise the survival of one or more persons, never letting them know *how* it came about.

One night I went online to find any occult websites that I could find that might afford me information or connection to anyone like Master Chip Ty Dick. A being named *Levi* had a site that proclaimed he knew the secrets to time travel. For a small shipping fee anyone could receive his discoveries about it. I ordered the report after checking his URL in the whois.org to see where he was probably located. Then seeing that he was overseas I optioned to download the documents.

THE HUNT FOR ALLIES

C. Van Heyden

Levi believes under hypnosis, by a trained operator, any person can go back in time and relive the past. He's done it many, many times, he says. But, I had done that already with Josh, achieved "time travel". What I needed was space travel and FAST. I emailed Levi a message about that. I got back, "Sorry, don't do space travel, AND anyway the worlds coming to an end." He added that there was a book he once read that talked about teleportation between worlds. He couldn't remember the title but the author's name had something to do with Alice In Wonderland and Nursery Rhymes. In my research up to that moment all my research was about teleportation on Earth, which even if it did exist for bodies, it would not get me home to Sellier. I had to locate that book.

First, I checked the World-Cat online, called a dozen bookstores in New York and Los Angeles, nothing. Each time the bookseller would say, "Lewis Carroll?" Lewis Carroll never wrote any books about teleportation or even mentioned it.

I hoped that being ignorant about doing one's taxes or what taxes were even about was passing. Also, stupidity about how things were made or done, and especially the mentality of those who, "Just do their job to get a pay check," were also on the decline—

which mentality I believe doesn't exist outside the reactionary need to defend oneself because of one's unenviable condition. Would it be a bad thing if a majority of the population were savvy about all the important things in life, and not just the things of day to day existence? How could it not. Children in elementary schools at the turn of the 20th Century studied two languages, usually Latin and sometimes Greek and one other and could write and speak them as well as proper English. And these were children that went back to working the farm or ranch when the summer season arrived. Math was a breeze, science held no mystery particularly. Children wanted to work and could work at an intelligent level until *once again* federal law was passed to *protect* them from exploitation. Shudder the thought, what that has engendered since.

Thoughts came to me rapidly: 'If I did locate it, would I understand it, and far more important could I build such a device except at astronomical cost?' Just like Clive Cussler in his stories has Pearlmutter, the man he goes to for arcane and obscure references— from books that are even greater in obscurity and arcaneness—I soon discovered such a person on campus. But before I could reach this person, a panic broke out amongst the senior students. It followed a report that the world in fact would be coming to end, for real this time, and the report included *scientific facts* which correlated with many ancient Mayan prophecies. This was the first time ancient and contemporary sciences congealed as one. Therefore, the illuminati of the university, the seniors of course and even some professors, were having meetings and calling for strict measures to see what could be done to save their insular world which they were sure this time was about to dematerialize.

This so disrupted class schedules and studying that the board of regents had to declare martial law. And not too unlike my experiences on Sellier with mass hysteria and civil commotion, I was not able to contact *my Pearlmutter*.

"Catherine?"

"I'm in the shower."
"OK love just wanted to make sure you were home. I've got some strange news to tell you when you are dry."

Catherine came bounding out of her bathroom naked, wet and with wide eyes, "You got all 'A's on your exams?"

"C-A-T-H-E-R-I-N-E...the term just started."

"Well, I...what's the strange news?"

"The world is not coming to an end." Catherine still naked and dripping water, "That's great! I was planning on taking us to dinner and then to bed for some fun early tonight." Catherine had landed a job with one of the administrators at the university, and I thought for sure she had gotten wind of all the foo-fa. Apparently not.

"Yeah, well I'm all for that plan, but what I said is true no matter what you hear or from who. The edges of the sun aren't going to explode into a shower of gamma rays that will knock out all electrical and electronic devices, equipment and generators and cast us into the dark ages again, and cause the poles to reverse."

"You look so cute when you get scientific with me." And back into the bathroom she went smiling and singing.

"Scientific", snapped back Elvis. 'Bloody show so far', he thought. He could not resign himself to just giving up and living the normal life. Out of 7 billion souls, refugees from other worlds, there must be not one but several who he could contact, and contact right now who knew enough to make a college try of getting back to his home planet. Getting their phone numbers or addresses and getting them in was the nut to crack.

Madame Chartreuse had aided him before in his efforts and she didn't fail him once. Could she be helpful, useful to contact more like himself was his question. Last time he asked Madame C. to locate other world beings who might have come from Sellier, she could only summon a ragtag posse of lost souls in limbo. But could she locate living beings as well, why shouldn't she? He hadn't asked her to do that, had he.

C. Van Hevden

LEADS FROM
MADAME C.

C. Van Hevden

"Madame C. this is Elvis. Since returning from China and starting my fifth semester, I have not been able to locate anyone who remotely has a reality on my home planet, Sellier, remember? I wonder if you could do some psychic research, and I'll pay you to contact someone on Earth living that I might reach for collaboration. Just let me know their names and where they are, and I'll take it from there. Bye."

At least he was doing something, instead of taking a back seat.

Catherine did as was predicted, she took Elvis to dinner, then to bed, and they resumed their relationship as though he had never been away.

As predicted, Madame C. responded within 24 hours with a list of names and locations. Elvis got to work and plotted out the closest ones, which turned out to be only one. He had sunk his last $200 in the effort which went to Madame C. The person he isolated as reachable—and this time he wanted a vis-à-vis—lived in Texas. Elvis needed it to be a one on one, since telephones are prey to tapping and conversations are subject to clandestine recordings. If he had to, he would hitchhike his way to Texas to meet this contact. That was a skill he had developed as a teenager and got to all places North, East and South from Layton.

He even hitchhiked West to his summer beach job and back and then downtown and back home when he lived in the suburbs. So good was he at doing it in those days, that one day a beautifully tailored, chic woman picked him up in a Mercedes open convertible and took him right to the spot he was headed towards.

This guy, Marcus was his name, nicknamed Marty, lived not far from San Antonio, one of the cities Elvis had visited in his sojourns away from Layton. The sojourns before he shoved off for China and Fengcheng province, where Josh was studying with taekwondo Master Chip Ty Dick. But Elvis couldn't just up and leave during semester; he had reports and mid-term exams in a few weeks, plus he could not afford to attract undue attention during his search and until he succeeded. Thanksgiving break lasted almost two weeks. That is when he would make his way East again.

BETTING WITH FORESIGHT

Hitchhiking was a definite failsafe plan, but he would still need funds for living expenses and for buying information and or help. Through Catherine he might get a loan from Frank Bishop, her father. That was dicey though. Why? Because she would want to know what the dough was for, and that would blow the whole plot. Catherine might still be a mite naïve but she was honest and she'd have to tell her dad what the money was for. Instead, Elvis decided he would lay a small wager on the football game coming up at home. He would use one of his special powers to see the future and make a profit while testing out the ability. This was being done with purpose, and therefore OK, so it had every chance of coming off. If it did work, he would do it again but with a larger sum, after he showed his classmates he could predict the exact final score. They would bankroll the following game bet.

Bingham had a decent football team but never had a truly winning season. Rival Cameron State probably would be victorious but not by much. The betting always included a bet on the spread of points. Elvis just looked and he saw 15 to 12 final score Cameron victorious. A bit screwy but that's what he saw. So he bet against his own team and put $25 on a three point loss to CS.

C. Van Heyden

"Hey Dickerson!"

"What's up Elvis?"

"Got a tip on the game this Saturday..."
"Thought you weren't a better."
"Only when I'm not certain of the outcome."
"You think we'll beat Cameron?"
"No, I think...no, I know we'll lose 15 to 12. and that's what's up. And you can tell your betting friends."

"I'll tell them, but I won't bet against Bingham. In fact, I've got them as a seven point winner this weekend. You sure you don't want to change your bet?"

"Not a chance."

"Where did this *tip* come from, or should I ask?"

"It's kosher. I've been doing some study in the occult, you know that Nostradamus thing we touched on in Philosophy."

"Yeah, but he took drugs before he got his predictions, and many were off quite a bit, although I admit some were on the money. You're not into drugs are you?"

"It's been all the rage on campuses since the '60's, but no I'm not into that. I do it by a method that you might call self-hypnosis."

"Well we'll see good buddy if you are Nostradamising well or not come Saturday."

Dickerson was a jock, and pretty decent basketball forward. He lacked the ability to jump and to dunk but he sure could fire from the outside. 'The Dick' as we named him, tried to get me to join the team, but at 6-2 I would be the shortest and I couldn't shoot worth a damn. He towered over me at 6-7 without the laces on.

The day of the game Saturday morning classes were suspended and the crowd was in the thousands, something new for Bingham. Bingham got the toss and out of the gate had a touchdown in about five minutes. It didn't bother Elvis, since the final score was already a foreseen fact. He knew it through and through. Then Cameron state scored two fairly easy touchdowns but no two-point conversions. For a second it rocked Elvis a bit since the half wasn't over; in fact there were fourteen more minutes of regulation play left. So, Bingham had seven and Cameron the twelve they would end the day with, since points can't be lost in football. Which gave Elvis a mischievous thought. Why couldn't they, and then he remembered a game like football he played on Sellier when he was growing up. It was almost the same except if a player intentionally injured another player the team lost its last score. And the team would lose its entire score if even one player gloated over a player of the opposing team receiving injury. Still another reason he wanted desperately to return to his home planet. It was much better than Earth.

When the second half began, threatening clouds, ominous clouds appeared seemingly from nowhere. Elvis had never been at football games in the rain, and the muddy conditions that were sure to ensue made him double think the whole scheme of his to get funds for visiting Texas during Thanksgiving. Water and pigskins do not mix well. Makes them slippery in the hands of quarterbacks, in the hands of the receivers trying to catch passes, in the hands of running backs causing them to fumble. It started to rain, and then it rained harder, so hard he could barely see the field and the players. Bingham needed to get only eight more points and NO MORE. Cameron needed to fumble the ball a lot and not make it near Bingham's end zone or a field goal would kill the wager, and his plans for Texas. The third quarter expired with no change in the score or the rain. It was hard to recognize the teams because their suits were getting completely muddy except the white numbers. But some of the defense players for Cameron showed the same numbers, like 88 was a line-backer and 88 was the tight end for Bingham. A short pass to the wrong 88 and....

This he could not let happen. As the clock wound down, and Bingham got more desperate to put the winning TD on the board, Elvis got a premonition that what he feared would happen was about to happen and Cameron would score instead of his team. He quickly went behind the bleachers and changed into a falcon. When the errant pass was thrown he flew right at it and deflected the ball, so it was not intercepted. In the rain few if any could tell what happened, it took place in an instant. Those that saw the deflection, who were close to the action said the ball wobbled. It was a bad pass. The quarterback saw it, knew something strange had happened but said nothing when he realized how close he had come to speeding the ball to the wrong 88.

Phew. Now Bingham with less than three minutes to play had to march forty yards to a TD or the game was lost, and Elvis was lost. Yet the conversion too had to be made; but right now, they had forty to make in the mud, no more passing unless it was a lateral.

C. Van Heyden

Dickerson showed up to gloat.

"So, you could be right Elvis, but you know Bingham hasn't scored in nearly three quarters. What makes you think they will now?"

"I could get into a long philosophic discussion with you Dick, but let's just watch and wait, OK?"

"Just to let you know, I did tell some of the frat boys and all of the betters in our circle that you were betting against Bingham."

"Glad you did, I'm looking forward to predicting the next football game as well."

"You know, if you are right the second time, you'll probably make a pile. But first you have to win today and at the score you predicted."

"I fully intend to do both."

Just then, the quarterback saw a golden opportunity and passed to the sideline flanker that was being loosely guarded since the past eight plays were runs. He flipped him the ball and the flanker ran it in for six points. Then the conversion and the game was as good as sealed at 15 to 12. Then,

"You were right about the score, but you were wrong about who won."

"No, I am right on both counts. After we talked I changed my bet Bingham would come from behind. The rain I didn't predict."

The Dick was speechless.

That night, Elvis took Catherine out to dinner with some of his winnings and told her all about the game and the bets. She dug football a lot, but couldn't get to the game, being staff she had to work Saturdays as well.

Now, to predict the next game and promote it loudly, repeatedly. Then a smooth exit come Thanksgiving. What story would he have to tell Catherine?

C. Van Heyden

WHITE LIE

C. Van Heyden

Why was he even studying for exams, did it matter, he was headed far away from Earth? His clairvoyance, his ability to assume other shapes, his clairaudience and who knows what other powers he would regain between now and when he departed, he would take with him. But, the thought lingered: what if he could not effect his departure from the information he was about to gain? He would have to make do until he could afford the capital to experiment, to discover or rediscover methods of interstellar travel. He was sure of that reality.

"Are you planning a trip Thanksgiving, love?"

"Catherine, it's for a company that I would like to work for. They're in Aerospace (which was true). They've been casting around for future technicians and my major is in space science, there's a fit."

"Isn't it a bit early to be talking employment?"

"Not when you realize that I could be finished early next year with all required subjects, graduate early, and they would fund my post graduate work on a pay-to-play basis."

"What does that mean?"

"Only, like football scouts for professional teams serve up inducements so a graduating athlete will sign with them and not another or rival team."

"That sounds pretty normal."

"It is, and when you think about it, it is simply good business if you want to hire the best for your company."

"Are they paying for your visit?"

"No, that is not something they will pay for since I'm not obligated in any way to sign a contract with them."

"You will be gone the whole recess?"

"Just about, since I want to do a thorough job of seeing what the opportunity offers."

"I won't mention that we talked about going away Thanksgiving?"

"You are right, I'm sorry. What we can do, and I would enjoy much more is if we had an even bigger getaway Christmastime, which is two and one-half weeks. How does that sound?"

"Sounds OK, as long as we fly to Palm Springs or stay in La Quinta, away from the cold."

"We can do that sure, I love Mt. San Jacinto. It will be warm down below and snow covered at the top should you get the hankering for a little Layton style frolicking in the white stuff."

"Not me."

"OK, we'll shop and eat at fine restaurants, within reason, and get lots of sun."

"That's me. And rent a Mercedes coupe?"

"Can your father lend you a couple of Franklins?"

"I'll squeeze him for it, and tell him it's his Christmas present."

"That a girl!"

Another phew.

It was true he had been interested in looking at the future after college, he had known of science based firms in San Antonio, Houston, Dallas etc. So, he was safe there, completely, or was he?

NEW ABILITIES & CLOSE CALL

C. Van Heyden

Elvis noticed another benefit, completely unexpected, from his confessions to Joshua: he could study very much more easily now, in fact he was a fast but careful student whereas before it was a true labor. This gave him extra time to search out the other names and locations Madame C. had supplied him, on the off chance that his Texas contact proved as useless as Levi did.

One was in New York, one in France in a town named something like marmalade in sound, one in South Africa and one in Peru. Seemed distribution was rather sparse for an Earth population of seven billion plus, or that's all that Madame C. had time to attend to.

R. C. Lexington in NY sounded mysterious, whereas his Texas contact's name was Marty. France was Mssr. Velatrobe, and South Africa was definitely not a South African but an Africaner named, Gingham. In Peru he would look up a woman known as Serena Amparo.

Elvis' excitement grew as he contemplated success. He was already hip to the UFO cover ups, the suppressed inventions of brilliant men by Neathandral thinking, reactionary monopolizers of oil interests. Inventions though that were harder and harder to destroy or swallow up because of the omnipresent Internet and all that its freedoms allowed with accent on new and unusual creations, and always better methods of doing something vital. He considered the impact of his thought: 'The proverbial genie has escaped out of the lamp, and no one, NO ONE or group could effectively stop the genie.'

Elvis contacted myself, the student Joshua had entrusted all of their session records to. I was the student who had divulged the private sessions to some of his student friends by way of Joshua's indiscretions. I had recanted later and decided to make up the damage he created by swearing to Joshua an oath to never gossip or pass on hearsay about another human being, no matter the justification. Since it was also a fraternity brother oath it was a reliable oath.

Elvis asked me to turn over the notes and records, which I did reluctantly. But Elvis saw that I was dejected. It was a big loss too, since I had achieved little in this life, and was rarely trusted. This oath meant that I was doing something vital and important and Joshua had trusted me without question once I gave his word to him. Elvis perceiving the pain of losing this trust, allowed me to be his new confessor providing that I take down Elvis' further confessions and adventures faithfully, combine all notes and session records into a manuscript. The data and experience that Elvis was after was too critical to Man not to make a permanent record of the vital parts. First, Elvis pored through those notes for any clue or piece of evidence that he may have forgotten since the sessions, in hopes he might have already even a better source for hooking up with another space traveler like himself. Nothing. He looked to promoting his next prediction for Bingham's football team.

Elvis true enough put his attention on the next game with Tempe Valley U. an out of conference team Bingham had never faced. He got that it would be a tie, 18 to 18. That didn't sound right but neither did 15 to 12. Nobody, has so far as he remembered wagered a tie. But it was possible. He went with it full force. Informed Dickerson and spread the word in his classes to a few other jocks he knew bet on the games.

Then he asked Dickerson and one of his buddies for $200 that would become $1400 at 7 to 1 odds. Netting him approximately 1200.00 since he'd kick in an extra $50 for the loan. The Dick said no he was thinking more like TVU winning, because he had scouted them, and he wouldn't bet against his own team. His buddy did go for the $200 after how it went down between Cameron State and Bingham. That was all Elvis needed really. Now it had to be 18 to 18 or one, he would lose the bet, and two he would lose credibility, and three he would owe $200 which he didn't have or would likely get anytime soon.

Saturday came and this time it was already raining with gusting winds. No matter, the conditions never decided the game or the score, once Elvis locked onto the future reading. Practically no one was at the game but then again that might not be a bad condition since it is widely known that a team's fans when they start rooting for their team to win and the other team or defense to mess up it can affect the score, sometimes in a major upset.

The first quarter, no score. Second quarter TVU almost made a TD on a trick play but the RB slipped on the turn up field and couldn't get his feet under him again. Half time came and went in a heartbeat since no band could play in the rain. 2nd half, score, zero zero. Again, Elvis for an instant got that doubtful flicker in his mind. 'With the rain present and not abating, no score through the first half, how were these two teams going to put up three TDs a piece in the same amount of time?'

He presumed all scores would be TDs and no extra points. Then he decided that if could predict the score, he could look into the future and predict the way the scores would occur. Simple. He got TVU scoring and kicking an extra point, then Bingham scoring and going ahead with a two point conversion, then a field goal. At that time the score would be 11 to 7 favor of Bingham. Dickerson said they are a better team, so the next score would be a touchdown by TVU with a two point conversion and they would lead 15 to 11. Then near the last two minutes or less TVU would be forced to kick a field goal on fourth down to ensure winning the game. That would leave scarcely a minute to play, but Bingham would pull a reverse in the mud that TVU tried and failed so they wouldn't be expecting it and Bingham would counter with a TD but no extra point, Bingham would come within a point of tying and two points of winning. Then take the tie with a point after since it was too tricky to try for a 2-pointer in muddy conditions and lose to a team that was favored when they could walk away with a draw. That's exactly what happened. Neither team could score in OT.

After paying back Dickerson's bud, he took Catherine out for dinner at the swankest restaurant in Layton. He could gloat, now that he had eleven hundred and fifty bucks and a reputation. Now, jocks and big betters were coming to him. The only problem is he didn't vitally need any more dough so he wasn't betting and if he wasn't betting and he didn't really need the money, it wouldn't work to forecast the next game; and that would lose a bunch of his friends and his friends' friends a ton of money. The best answer was to tell Dickerson and his friends that it was too dangerous putting himself into an hypnotic trance to predict scores, and that for his own health he would not continue to do it. This angered many of the betters who wanted a sure thing, especially the ones who hung back waiting to see if lightning struck twice. In the end it blew over as a hoax and most of the betters called it pure beginner's luck.

MARTY

C. Van Heyden

Elvis also scored well academically, with A's on both his aeronautical physics and thermodynamics papers, plus a 94% on his calc examine. He had given up on locating that book on teleportation, at least for the time being, but he had an intuition that his understanding of these subjects he was studying and some input from the right sources he would figure it all out himself as to how to make his way back to Sellier. And as hoped Catherine wangled a promise of $200 from her father giving Elvis breathing room should he vacate all his earnings in Texas and come back with only change in his pockets.

He would go by Greyhound, keeping more of his funds so that if he needed to buy privileged or confidential information he could do so with fewer worries. Elvis even packed several meals into a picnic cooler to save on restaurant food and tips.

The man he would meet, Marty, said he'd meet him at the bus station in San Antonio and take him to a hotel, Best Western class. When he arrived, he met a squat somewhat rotund man about fifty with thinning hair, but a large smile and comforting eyes.

"How went the bus trip?"

"You're Marty?"

"Yep, always have been."

"It went fine, I've been out this way before."

"So, you know San Antone, do you?"

"Pretty good, I spent a week here last year and got to see a lot of real estate, you might call it."

"Well, then I won't bother to show you around, we can just meet tomorrow morning for breakfast, and you can get some rest from what I believe was a twenty hour bus ride, correct?"

"Closer to twenty-two, do you ride Greyhound?"

"No, I just looked at the schedule for your arrival, and it told me duration of travel time."

"It was a long one, but the seats are comfortable and of course anyone can sleep if they want. For myself, I just napped now and then. But I would like to get a fresh start in the morning, and get into my hotel room for a shower."

"Sounds very good, I'll see you in the morning. BW

has a great breakfast in a not so bad restaurant downstairs."

"See you then Marty."

"See you tomorrow Elvis."

Elvis liked hotels, motels. He loved not having to clean up messes or worry about fresh towels and fresh sheets, they were just there. And cable T.V. was always included. He tried to catch the results of the last game of the season for Bingham, but it was too late, the sports station had stopped reporting scores earlier. So, he showered a hot shower and hopped into bed. It wasn't long before the sawing of logs could be heard softly.

Next morning was a beautiful one with fleecy clouds and a few gusts of wind to make the fall leaves scurry into small piles. Dressing warmly, Elvis went downstairs for breakfast to meet Marty, it was 8:00 AM.

Marty signaled him over to a table in the rear of the restaurant.

"How was your rest?"

"Quite good, I always fall asleep faster on fresh clean sheets. It reminded me of a feather bed I slept in, in Syracuse one night at this adorable bed and breakfast. After having a scrumptious meal complete with fresh vegetables out of the garden I was conveyed to this bedroom that sported a large four-poster with down pillows and comforter, even the mattress was down I think. I fell asleep in a minute."

"I'm glad you're rested. I'm glad because what I'm about to reveal to you will probably stand your hair on end like during a thunder storm's lightning."

"I think I can take it."

"Here goes then..."

"Wait, is this going to be verifiable data?"

"Seeing is believing, right?"

"That's what I'm looking for."

"As I was saying, I travel a bit. In my travels I made it to the Bosphorus area, do you know where that is?"

"Vaguely...in Europe?"

"Not precisely. It's near the Dardanelles and connects the Black Sea with the Mediterranean, and its fame is that it is a place of legend. One of the legends is it was impassable because of giant rocks that were awash in its waters. What I discovered, since it had been a hobby of mine to climb mountains, is that there is some kind of transfer point for beings outside this galaxy there."

"By what you're saying, this find is not known about at all?"

"Only those who are looking for it will find it, that's what I am saying."

"Continue."

"Well it is well hidden in a mountain pass, and I searched. Yeah did I search a long time to find it. You see I believe, let's say I have had a suspicion about extra-terrestrials for as long as I can remember. Something happened when I was young that made me remember a past existence, and it scared me somewhat but not enough to shut off the memory. I was six."

"Marty, when we talked briefly by phone, I told you why I wanted to see you, but I didn't tell you how I came to have your name and number. You never asked either."

"That's because I can see a person telepathically and know whether they are telling me the truth or not. And I've had that ability since I was six or younger."

"So, you knew at once that I was not from Earth?"

"I didn't say that, only that your request was legit, and not some plot to discredit me or trap me."

"I got your name from a medium, a medium who has checked out completely for real, completely capable in her art."

"I don't doubt it for a moment. There are persons in this world who have such abilities we never suspect, and I for one having telepathic skills I would be the first to embrace the notion that a good number of individuals must have similar qualities."

"Tell me more about this *place* you discovered."

"The approach and entrance are high up enough to discourage most climbers, and if you have ever seen the sheer walls that mountain goats climb up and down with no fear, then you know the kind of terrain I'm talking about."

"Yes, I get what you're telling me, rough country."

"Precisely. So that if you have the heart—the determination to arrive—you'll get there in one piece. Once there you'll think there's "nothing here"; you'll think that, but you'll be very wrong. I brought a metal detector and a Geiger counter. And with those instruments I got readings way off the dial for both. That's the other danger. Radioactive material."

"How did you survive it?"

"I almost didn't. I did get sick. But fortunately like a G-O-O-D boy scout I came prepared. Since I was carrying a Geiger-counter, naturally I brought a lotion containing aloe vera and calendula which is effective against radiation burns. Only good for low doses. Which is why I got sick. Unless you can operate in a water sealed uniform, like a diver's wet suit you will probably get sick too. But you'll recover after a few weeks, if you don't stay too long."

"Sounds very adventurous."

"Oh, it is *very* adventurous. I aged about five years."

"What do you want in exchange for the exact location and maps?"

"Nothing, now that we've met. So, you say you're not from here—where then?"

"A planet called Sellier and it's in the direction of the Constellation Boötes and very distant."

"Well, I make no promises, but I'll provide you with exact directions once you land in Turkey."

"What did you see when you got inside the mountain?"

"I'm going to let you find that out for yourself, you wouldn't believe me if I tried to tell you. Remember, don't stay around there long."

"Not a hint, so I won't be charred by the experience if it's too much?"

"I can tell you that you will see contraptions that couldn't possibly be made by earth men, and you'll hear things that you have never heard before, so also take ear plugs. I didn't think of that, and it's another reason I got sick."

"OK, so that's it I go and find the place you've been describing to me. What of contacting the beings?"

"I don't know about that. I wasn't looking to get off this planet anytime soon, as I presume you are."

"OK, did you see any of them?"

"Yes, I did, and they are not too different than you or I. But they don't communicate with their mouths, get it? So, if you're not telepathic you wouldn't be able to reach them."

"That poses a serious problem to me. But it's my problem. Let me have the data and I'll keep it secret.

You know I will."

"Meet me tomorrow here, same time."

FOX AND FALCON

BANK ROBBERY

Marty didn't have the true data he was looking for, only where to go to get it or to get back to Sellier. Still a long shot and far away.

When Marty handed over the maps and directions, he also gave Elvis the name of the radiation lotion and where to buy some. Elvis wanted to pay him for his time, but Marty wouldn't go for it. Marty would be happy if he succeeded, or if Elvis didn't at least destroy the maps and directions and let him know that he did.

By simple math, Elvis calculated that he would need about four times the bankroll he had to launch an expedition overseas. That meant working all summer and if lucky have enough to start in the fall next year.

'God', he thought. 'I just don't know if I can wait that long.'

In the next days, Elvis made his way back to Layton. But before he did, a bank robbery had occurred only blocks from his hotel, done in the manner of the old west too. Seems two men with kerchiefs over their faces up to their eyes came in to the San Antonio Federal Bank building with six-guns blazing, shot a few tellers in the shoulders to make sure no one went for the buzzers under the counter, and made off with $200,000.00 in bills and traveler's cheques. The police had no leads and no clues. Elvis stepped in and offered his services, telling the chief detective on the case to call Sheriff Bradford in Layton for corroboration of his skills. Having done so, Elvis was sworn in as a temporary deputy of the Bexar County Sheriff. He went right to work at the bank putting his attention on the time the alleged bank robbers had entered the premises and shot up the joint. In a few minutes, he was able to perceive that the assistant manager was in on the heist. Normally, the vault would not be open, but this time the assistant manager had contrived to have it so when the gun men barged in and demanded the money.

He relayed this info to the detectives on the case and they brought in the assistant manager who folded after only an hour of interrogation.

This time, Elvis was rewarded *and* cited in the newspapers for his commendable action.

'Chalk up one more good deed for posterity, even though it was a type of negative gain,' mused Elvis. It seemed to him at that moment that positive gain should be his major thrust in life, not merely counterbalancing or correcting bad things. What were the positive things in life? Inventions, discoveries, art, manufacturing, harvesting—and of course planting first—education leading to proficiency and productivity...there were lots more.

Elvis added the $500 CD reward the bank gave him to his total funds, and headed back to Layton a winner. Home, he relayed all the details of his trip, substituting Marty's name with various contrived names of heads of personnel departments and told Catherine mainly about the reward for helping apprehend the evil-doers in San Antonio.

"So, did you land a position?"

"Not exactly, but I got a good lead. It seems there was a bit of hype I didn't quite pick up on originally at college when I heard about the pay-to-play offer."

"How so?"

"Seems I didn't get all the info I needed, and it turns out there's a big investment on my part starting with a change of location at my expense before anything more happens."

"You mean they want *you* to move at *your* expense to Texas before they sign you on?"

"Pretty close. That's the job market these days. They had too many promising candidates wash out in the first six months, breaking their contracts. They want to see tangible production first."

"OK, so you're not in a hurry to finish college then?"

"That's the size of it my sweet."

"Can we talk about Christmas now?"

"Sure, I was hoping we would."

FORTUNE TELLING

Christmas came, and Christmas left, but the hunger Elvis felt didn't. Even the thought of robbing a bank came to him in a sheer moment of desperation, but he laughed it off as absurd. 'In the old days' he was reminded 'a guy could get aboard a tramp steamer to practically anywhere, as long as he was willing to experience stinking quarters, sea sickness, bad food, hard deck labor or freezing night watches.'

He had had such an experience, which when reviewing brought up a confession, and perhaps it is where the errant thought of robbing a bank came from. So, he wrote it down and mailed it to me (James): "Put in the record that in and around 1930ish I was made assistant purser on a steamer out of Boston Harbor bound for South Africa. They gave me a job of doling out the pay in envelopes for the crew, and I managed to embezzle several hundred dollars. By the time they found out, I had jumped ship in Durban and signed up with another outbound vessel heading back to New York."

The new year brought Elvis to face another semester with no hope of getting enough free time to procure a job where he could earn the wherewithal to get over to Eurasia and locate the teleportation station. Catherine was hinting at engagement again, after a very intimate and prolonged Christmas celebration with Elvis as her only consort. Too bad Elvis was above it, he could easily have Catherine take photos of her semi-naked and in the buff and get a spread in Playboy, then take his cut as her manager. Exploiting women was still a *sous réserve de lombre.*

Then quite accidentally Elvis became aware of something he was already doing that others would enjoy and that he could charge for: fortune telling. Only it wouldn't be long range fortune telling. More like what the wagering on football games consisted of, all short-term and all to make others some extra cash *or* better prevent them from losing it. So they wouldn't mind parting with some cash up front, and he would be guaranteed a good deal of repeat and new customers without advertising, once he got it started. He'd put an ad in...not the local paper but one in the big city in a cheap local paper and see if he got any bites, similar to how Madame C. promoted. He could do all by telephone and use an Internet email for transfer of funds.

He placed an ad in the San Francisco Bee stating, "Want to make sure you never place a losing bet at the casinos or on football? Call for free demonstration. Anonymity guaranteed." And he started receiving requests almost immediately. He was doing it, so he could get the necessary funds collected to pay for his expedition so it was ethical, meaning it benefitted more than it disadvantaged.

Within a month he had the four grand he needed for plane fare, mountain climbing gear which he'd purchase when he arrived, for food and hotel accommodations and spare in case of injury or_____? Now, to clone himself and make his way to the threshold to the orient, the land of the Arabian nights and magic, Turkey. Elvis realized it was still a shot in the dark and that more than likely he would have to return, so he bought a round-trip ticket for May, the soonest year-end exams would be over, and he could exit. This time he would blatantly tell Catherine the truth, but only enough to make for a clean departure.

FOX AND FALCON

COUNSELOR TO
THE LOST

Elvis hadn't done much in his efforts to improve the lots of others, since returning from the orient, just that one incident in San Antonio, which again was *negative gain.* He told me that if he had a great deal of money he would open a foundation as many wealthy and famous persons do, Yet, even so that kind of contribution wouldn't net him any tangible increase in powers, and that was his last thought on the matter. He had nearly five months left in which to exercise his talents, where doing so would somehow lift another's life from stagnation or even, if it mattered, a normal good level to an even much higher level. That would be a *positive* gain—much like individuals who take up chess and sharpen their mental skills and even their ability *to play a game.*

Predicting when not to place bets fell obliquely into the above category, when it was done for the average Joe, but wasn't strong enough to cause any release of his other latent abilities. Doing it for the compulsive gambler, who Elvis carefully tried to screen and eliminate was no gain at all. He considered that a loss. Now, it occurred to Elvis that one of the major downfalls of individuals, as he saw it, was indecision. Even above average intellects were deficient in the courage to take action based upon a firm decision, with the decision ascendant in all cases. We can cite Joshua's decision to relocate to an unknown province and unknown environment in China *after* he made the decision to reverse his life goals, a major decision in truest sense. This was an excellent area, a fertile area for Elvis to explore.

There were many students that he knew that were just going through the motions without any solid goal in mind as to what they were going to do with their education, or for that matter with their lives. There were school career counselors, sure, but these cats were often just senior students in their last year at the university, and some if not many were in the same boat, trying to help themselves find direction as much as to help the freshman and sophomores. I know, I was one. The standard tests for aptitude told only where a student has abilities not which life's goals he or she should strive the hardest to achieve. It takes...it takes whatever Joshua got a hold of to settle completely which path to take and to pull out all the stops, no matter what.

Since Elvis could pick up the thoughts of a person when in their presence. He began counseling one student at a time, one student he selected that he liked, and thought would be fairly easy to counsel. No druggies, no criminal types, at least not at first. For free. He started with me, since I knew Joshua.

I was not an easy first. He tried to get me to recall a previous existence and all I got was blackness. Then he asked me if there was anything in the blackness that wasn't entirely black. After a while something showed, very hazy and I couldn't describe it. So, then he asked if I could recall a past death. Now *that* was something I could get something on and from there we were off and running as the saying goes. Since this is not my confessions, I'll just tell you what came of it that was very satisfying and liberating for myself. I had always had a belief that everyone was a *phony,* meaning no one was every really sincere. It was all a show, a put on, feelings, expressions, manners, the whole bit. That ended. Naturally I had told my parents that I was going to college to become an architect like my father was, so they would pay for everything; when, in fact I have always wanted to be a film-maker / producer, making the blockbusters and living the high life. I was being the phony that everyone else I thought was.

Next up was Ted Larkin. Seems Joshua had put him and a few of his friends through the grinder about past life existences. Ted even got sick during his sessions, though he wouldn't tell Josh about it. Elvis got him, and he too was a toughy. But, finally he came up with a string of previous lives and if he were here I'd ask him if it was alright to divulge what he saw and learned in that one session. He similar to Joshua up and left Layton.

Left for New York City, and told me he was going on Broadway and act for the rest of his life on the stage. Frankly that scared me because he looked nothing like an actor nor did he, when I knew him, have the personality of an actor. Ted, if anything had been a jerk-off and very cynical. Then, sometime around Valentines' Day, Elvis quit, he was burnt out he told me. He had salvaged probably a dozen students at Bingham. So that part of his life came to an end.

Instead of continuing in hopes of his quest for full return of his native powers, Elvis decided to begin his egress. First, he dropped hints with Catherine about the coming overseas expedition, not mentioning its true purpose but only that he was interested in traveling throughout Europe and Western Asia to fulfill a lifelong dream he had. Catherine of course could not be included since she had work beyond the college semester plus the way Elvis told it he would be moving so fast to cover *so much ground* that it would be uncomfortable to invite another along. He could only operate by himself at that speed. Since C. knew he had taken off the previous summer on a tour of the states this was believable. But it wasn't all right with her.

From Feb 14th to May 7th, final exams nothing else of note transpired for Elvis or Catherine. The day came when he kissed her goodbye at the airport and told her he would try to send a letter or call at least once each week. When he landed in Istanbul airport Elvis made his way to a tiny hotel Marty had included in his notes, a hotel that was the same when he had landed there. Elvis was packing about a hundred pounds of climbing equipment and special high protein food that climbers use to stay strong on long treks. If it had been in the winter, he would have had to also take with him a Coleman stove for sure heating at night to keep from freezing. Still, the nights in the high mountains, Marty told him, would not be comfy, so bring winter weight gear. The maps supplied by Marty were clear, showing relative altitudes of mountains and where there were dense forests to avoid. Getting to the base of the mountain would require hiring a car and driver since no public transportation, train, boat or plane landed anywhere near them. The one thought that plagued Elvis was falling and injuring himself and no one was there to help him. He might drag himself to safety, but he wouldn't acquire the hidden entrance that he came seven thousand miles to investigate.

Arriving in sight of his goal, he decided to rest and get plenty of it at the Gurang Hotel where his

English was just barely understood by the inn keeper. The next morning he stopped by the local police office to let the chief there know that he was a mountain climber and that he would be scaling one of two mountains on either side of the Bhanghi Pass. This way he would have a chance if he didn't come back in one piece since a search party would cover both, and at the same time would not give away the location of the teleportation station. There was one section of the climb where Elvis had to use pitons, especially designed spikes, that when forced into the rock face made a hand hold and a step in shear walls. Only once before had he any experience with this climbing device and again it was the warmer weather that made him confident that he could use them well to get past that barrier.

The town at 3,000 feet altitude left only 7,000 feet to climb to where the map detailed the hidden entrance. But the last 1,000 feet was shear rock. This formidable deterrent and its remote location had kept the teleportation site's existence utterly unknown. Marty had marked the map with unique symbols to show where he had successfully navigated the treacherous climb many years ago. Elvis got through the underbrush and across small streams without incident, but when he saw the beginning of the rock face 9,000 feet up from sea level he had to draw some deep breaths. 'It could all end here' was his impression then. But even the 6,000 ft climb to that façade was more than he had previously climbed. It took five hours to finally reach it. Scratched and his hands sore in spite of special climbing gloves he looked upward and spied the peak that he had to acquire to get to the entrance. It was 2 o'clock in the afternoon. If he was successful by 5:00 PM he would be there, with enough time to do a preliminary recon and come down to a manageable camping spot before night fall.

Elvis checked his gear, pitons, hammer, harness, carabiners, climber's rope that he would tie off in steps as he ascended—in case he should fall—it would slow and break his rapid descent. And he made doubly sure he was carrying the aloe cream for radiation burns. It began well for the first fifty feet. Then an eighteen inch shelf appeared overhead to complicate his upward progress. Managing that without a hitch he ascended another 300' and rested. It was 3:30 PM and four hours until sunset, another hour to the summit. He was running behind. As he told it, he got giddy as he reached the 900 foot mark of the thousand he needed to scale. His strength was flagging. His morale was sky-high, but his expectations were tremulous, remembering what Marty told him, "You'll see contraptions that couldn't possibly be made by earth men". He not only wanted to see these machines, he wanted to cast himself off Earth in one of them.

At the highest point of the shear rock there was a fissure, large enough for a typical human to pass through. Large enough if the man *or woman* wasn't claustrophobic and if not wearing protective clothing didn't mind getting scratched up a lot. Elvis came out on the other side to a long corridor within the mountain top and he followed it to the room that was mentioned in text on his map. As he approached he removed his climbing gloves but plugged his ears with stops, just as Marty directed. Elvis was several hundred feet inside the mountain where no one would find him if this was the end of him. Faintly, then louder as he walked further came screeching sounds and banging sounds. By the time he was at the threshold of the space that contained the teleportation system, he knew Marty was right. Once at Hoover Dam, on a field trip, he had experienced the sound of the dynamos at the fifth level down, and they were frightfully loud even when wearing ear protection given out by the tour guides. As he told it, "I must have walked through an air vent to the teleportation area, because I was looking down at an enormous contraption made of steel. A contraption which resembled nothing I had seen in my life nor in my sessions with Joshua. It seemed to be afloat in a lake of mercury. I gathered that the *mercury* was cooling the mammoth machine. As for the operators...I can only say that they were human sized with appendages like us but not with human faces and feet or hands, and definitely not with ears. Remembering Marty's comment about telepathic communication I sought to get as close to the main body of workers while sending out a gentle thought that I am also not from Earth and needing help getting back to my home planet."

BOSPHORUS

C. Van Hevden

Nothing. Perhaps these were workers only, the overseers remote or hidden watching and commanding. Marty said he could pick up their communication, but he didn't say whether they intercepted his. Elvis tried again, sending the simple thought, 'I am not from Earth and I'm needing help getting back to my home planet.'

That triggered something. He hadn't mentioned the name of the planet previously. Since this was a departure point, as well as ingress point for other planets where beings lived, it made some sense that the true names of planets, that would not change over time, and if known, would be permanently entered into the coordinates of the giant transporting devices. Remember, Elvis with his climbing gear on and sun goggles above his eyebrows looked a bit strange himself, his ropes and harness left at the entrance to the fissure.

Elvis began to experience an unpleasant sensation all over his body. Suddenly it came back to him that he was supposed to not linger on this spot. He took off his climbing gloves and noticed a reddening of his skin. Radiation. He realized that radiation sickness doesn't befall one immediately, and the evidence that he would be sick was in clear sight. He moved quickly to outermost perimeter of the teleportation site and headed back through the corridor vent tunnel. Emerging from the tunnel he found fresh mountain air that stimulated his senses even more. Now he could feel the pain of his burning hands and face which went unfelt inside the cavern because he was distracted first by the noise, the sights and then by the colossal apparatus and workers around it, moving as if controlled.

It was 6:25 when Elvis checked his chronometer attached to his belt. He thought that he could not climb down nor reverse his ascent below the sheer face before it got dark in less than an hour and a half. If he stayed at the fissure he had a small area where he could lie down, but he didn't know and didn't think that he could stay warm enough throughout the night. Winds were blowing better than 20 mph through the crevasse he had just emerged from to escape being burned to death radioactively. If he stayed he ran the risk of needing to be rescued if his strength was not up to retracing his steps back to the point he started climbing the rock face. The only comforting thought left was that he had scaled to the top of the mountain, found the alleged teleporting station and if lucky will live to try again.

He decided he would repel down in stages tying off a double length of rope at each stage and looping it through his harness, a tricky maneuver even for well-trained climbers. Then pull the rope as a single chord through the pulley above and attach to another pulley and continue down 'til he reached level ground. Before the start of his descent he pulled a bottle of the special lotion from his back pack and soothed as much as he could his face and hands. Lastly, he trekked lower to a spot he noted on the way up that was tree sheltered away from the wind, where he could bed for the night. With this accomplished he rested.

In the early morning, stiff and hungry, Elvis rose and plied his way back to the Gurang Hotel and showered and rested again. Upon rising Elvis went in search of a library and municipal records vault. It seemed to him that it must be impossible for such a station to be operating close, albeit hidden, to human civilization that there had not been some contact, no matter how clandestine, at some time during the past thirty to who knows how many years. If there had been, and in all likelihood should have been, there must be a go-between, an earth contact person or persons. 'Surely if something happened where a worker or other alien up there got badly hurt they would need a full-fledged hospital and staff to take care of them, or did they die as just another drone bee would, immediately replaced by another dispatched through the great machine?' It was this sole thought of a go-between (planted or otherwise) which lead him further: Elvis, no matter what, wasn't returning home empty handed.

Elvis had not gotten sick as Marty had. Checking his entire peripheral nervous system (skin) he found only moderate redness under his clothes. With the salve he was back to battery and ready to extend his stay in Turkey. Elvis had an unusually strong constitution, another side benefit derived from his confessions.

Elvis looked only for old folks, villagers that had been around a long, long time. Individuals that with a little cajoling and a few innocent bribes would cough up the evidence he knew had to exist.

'Bharabhas' (BHAR-A-BAS) was his name. He had lived in the village all his 89 years. Through wind and sunburned lips, he whispered of a being he met a half century ago; a being he felt was a stranger to this planet. Referring to that entity as Throgg, since he had never learned of his identity, Bharabhas told Elvis of that day. And Elvis relating to me (James) we come to revelation of how the being and the station came to be hidden all these years: a field of force. Like a jelly-fishes transparent flesh, surrounding the mountain cancelling out any invasive transmissions in either direction, perceptible to no one. Throgg appeared that day and only one other time in recollection. He gave Bharabhas a token to remember their conversation, and he showed it to Elvis. But he would not let Elvis hold it or even examine it. Elvis drew a picture of it and this is what he drew:

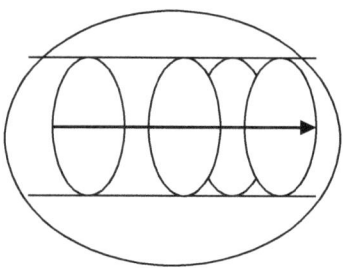

Elvis told me that when he had drawn this figure he was reminded of a play—no, a musical his father told him he'd seen when he was young and liked a long time ago named STOP THE WORLD I WANT TO GET OFF, that had never been revived really, like so many other musicals from on Broadway in N.Y. And a song reverberated in his head at the same time:

Why don't we sing this song altogether
Open our minds let the pictures come,
And if we close our eyes together
Then we will see where we all come from.

It left me wondering, if that was a universal symbol for teleportation. It left Elvis with an unsatisfied hunger. Elvis continued searching quietly the village for another "Throgg" but found no one. This was the lowest he'd been since leaving Josh and Master Chip Ty Dick in China. He dared not go back to the station without a suit of protection against the radiation. He hadn't called Catherine in five days, and it was unlikely she would be able to cheer him, what with the hot weather coming and them apart again like last summer.

He tried calling Marty, no answer, and gave up. There wasn't anything Marty could do—that's why he had given Elvis the maps with details. Marty had *had* his adventure and was on to other matters. Then it dawned on him. Change shape and go there as a falcon. Go there and stay there in very short periods so as not to burn up. Get as much familiarity with the operation, look for overseers, look for actual beings arriving or departing: he hadn't seen any yet. And minimally discover how it was that the drones could work in that environment at all. Then, acquire a suit back home capable of withstanding that roentgen level. He wouldn't go home empty handed after all.

TELEPORTATION STATION

Navigating the passage he'd come back through was tougher as a falcon, winds had increased. Elvis gets to the enormous room where the teleporters are and no one is there. Funny thing is, being a bird, the first thing Elvis does is look for other birds that might have flown in as he did, and to see if they were dead.

It occurred to him then that the room saw action only when a transfer was in progress. He must have come in last time right near when a transfer was ending, and the workers were shutting down. But now he could get around to many more locations within the cavern and much faster. Where was the central control? Where did they eat, sleep, exercise?

It didn't matter, he hadn't been able to reach them telepathically. Likely the drones were sequestered, living in shielded rooms that he could not invade. And that's how the drones, anyone, kept from getting radiation sickness or worse dying. They worked in short spurts, plus a natural immunity to small doses built up over the years. He flew high, hundreds of feet from the floor and found the control area. Through shielded glass extremely thick he made out many signs and inscriptions. All were in shapes and figures more bizarre than hieroglyphics. He was despondent. As he told me in his own words, "I have always been resourceful Josh, tenacious, capable of discovering a way through any morass, any problem. But I am completely stymied here." He was so despondent he thought I was Josh! And I wrote him back, "EA, don't give in. Look at the great things you have done for others, and the contributions. You are a saint in my mind." Even this did not cheer him. Then, Elvis popped the question: What have you learned from Master Dick? I fudged. I told him, "True I was progressing past the first stages of my training, certainly his new house was built, and a beauty it was. Master Dick had already taught me many things not just Tae. But nothing about his previous existences nor about interstellar travel. No, these were not part of the curriculum for the making of a Martial Arts Master."

Elvis began his retreat. Packed his bags and traveled first to Istanbul for his flight. But, before take-off sold the climbing gear (slightly used) back to the shop there where he bought it. Headed back to Layton.

ANOTHER FAILURE

C. Van Heyden

Thinking he'd be gone all summer Catherine was ecstatic and bubbling with joy to see him, meeting him at the airport. Elvis tried to hide his disappointment from her.

"What happened, what was your impressions of Europe?" chirped Catherine.

"I hit some very rugged country, met only very rural people, did some mountain climbing, and that's pretty much all that happened."

"But, didn't you want to tour over there?"

"I did, but factually I got sick and it sucked the fun out of my plans."

"That's a real shame. But, in celebration of your return I have prepared a little special home coming for you...Rob Dickerson, who you know and his girlfriend Sherry, plus Olivia my new best friend. So, there will be more girls than guys."

"When is it?"

"Tomorrow night!"

"Tomorrow night?...I don't think I'll be in the mood, but I'll give it my best."

"After tonight, I guarantee you'll be in the mood."

Elvis had all summer to debate with himself what he was going to do: now that he had half the total funds left that he started with. No one to commiserate with, and no one to tell of his success to either because he had none. He finally settled on, and concluded, to work all summer to fund further sorties, and to procure a radiation proof suit that could be carried lightly back to "the site", as he thought of it now. And if very lucky recover his climbing gear at the same cost as he traded it.

But Elvis hated the mundane and repetitive game of *looking for a job*, even if only a summer job. He'd rather be asked if he'd like to work by a professor, or businessmen in town, considering his temporal and supernal abilities together. So, he thought it.

At the party, Olivia gave him a scare. She approached Elvis and asked him if he had heard of a guy on campus counseling students in private with a strange kind of method. Elvis evaded, "Where did you hear that?"

"My boyfriend told me."

"Well, was it good for him?"

"Very good as he told it, but wouldn't go into details."

"It's privileged information is why."

"That's what I thought too."

"So, Olivia, he's lucky and you're lucky too, right?"

"Why am I lucky too?"

"Because, you're his girlfriend, and if he's much better off, then you being in his closest circle...."

"Oh, I get it, it rubs off as the saying goes."

"Precisely right. Have you wanted counseling?"

"Hmm...it occurred to me I might get something out of it."

"Well, I will tell you something private, and ask you to keep it that way."

"Oh, I will do that."

"I happen to know the fellow, and he taught me what he knows."

"He did, really?"

"Why don't we go into the next room, I'll tell Cathy you want to talk to me about something personal in private."

"OK."

Elvis and Olivia went into a session. When Olivia came out she was aglow. Catherine couldn't help noticing.

"Whatever did you talk about in there?"

"Gee Catherine, we went in there for privacy, you know? But I will say that your man here is quite knowledgeable."

"Yeah, he's quite a guy, *my* guy." And Catherine smiled warmly.

Elvis knew he was taking a big chance, since best friends tell all, or they are not best friends. He would find out right away, one way or the other. He bet, he hoped Olivia would stay true to the covenant he made with all his applicants and not divulge any details of her session.

C. Van Heyden

SUMMER JOB

C. Van Heyden

Saturday morning, Elvis got a call from Frank Bishop, Catherine's father. Frank worked for a top flight design company in San Diego called MB Design Center. Frank asked Elvis what he was doing this summer and if he needed a job. Yes in caps. There was an opening for an engineering student with drafting skills that opened up suddenly due to a staff member having to leave for the East coast to attend his ailing parents. Probationary of course, but paid well if he lasted. Elvis faxed his transcripts immediately, and with Frank's endorsement he got the OK to start the position. He could finish his credits for graduation come the Fall, giving personnel time to find a full time replacement.

Plans suddenly leaped into view in front of Elvis. He would take the job, commute to Layton on the weekends, find a cheap motel for accommodations and save the bucks. SAVE THE BUCKS. This became a mantra, a mantra that would take him either back to the teleportation station or to CHINA or both.

Catherine was miffed, but not intensely so. Elvis and she could cuddle and spoon on the weekends, and she could have Olivia over during the week for girl things. Plus, Elvis pretended he hated to leave her which made it all the better.

With his learning rate so rapid now, although he had had only a smidgen of drafting experience, he knew he would excel.

Elvis called some 800 numbers, found a store within a hundred miles that stocked radiation protection suits. He got quotes for the range from least to most expensive. Made a record of those figures. Then he called around to several rent-a-car lots and asked what each could do for a college guy commuting to and from San Diego. Pitting one against another he finally arrived at a monthly rate lower than corporate, about 600 per month, and he could still have his pick of the brand and model. Then he long-distance called a few motels near MB Design and got quotes, telling the managers the same as the rent-a-car shops. He noticed how easy it was to get discounts, sometimes huge, by telling factually the purpose. People, the vast majority he calculated, mainly wanted to help other people if they could. Not the way his father or anyone close to him saw it when he was growing up.

Things were definitely going his way now. But as he told me.

"Damn it! I left out clothes. MB Design was a suit and tie business. That's going to set me back quite a bit at first. Two suits, shirts, new shoes, probably two pair and ties. About $1,000 to look right and for enough shirts to go one week in the summer without laundry detail. That's my first four weeks minus food, car and rent."

If anyone could, Elvis could stretch a dollar so it looked like soft taffy. The real excitement was in the fact that he would be around full-fledged engineers, experts in metallurgy and structural physics. Who knows perhaps one of them might even have knowledge of how to build a teleportation device or be working on one now.

His farewell night with Catherine, he reported, was exquisite. He also discovered during their intimate moments that Olivia had kept her promise.

C. Van Heyden

CHARLES LEXINGTON

C. Van Heyden

MB Design Center was huge, amazingly large. Three individual four story buildings linked by glass tunnels. Elvis shared an office with two other draftsmen, Chuck and Rob. They welcomed him grandly and made him feel accepted. They were in shirt sleeves. But that changed the minute they had to go out or attend any meetings in the building. The day Elvis had dropped in on Stockton the previous summer to get the dope on him, he wore sunglasses as the floral delivery man, so now no one would recognize him.

The draftsmen worked closely with the design department, so Elvis was in contact with Frank Bishop a lot. This gave him a secure feeling in a strange environment even though he was warmly welcomed by others. Frank's speed was legendary at MB. Draftsmen could expect one to three design drawings a day from colleagues of Frank, but Frank poured in designs in batches, sometimes ten at a time. Designs from models modifying inside door panels, trunk spaces, dash accessories, outside details having to do with roof rake and grille patterns, wheel hub spacing and look. There were fourteen models for which these and other specifications changed during the design and modeling stages, not to mention for heavy machinery also produced by MB. So there was a constant flow of documents back and forth between departments until the final designs for each model were approved by top management.

Elvis was liking his situation very much. He knew what he was really there for, and he knew that it was all right to be doing it. As predicted his first, 2nd and 3rd pay checks went to room & board, car and gas and clothes which he bought each week until he had a wardrobe. The first week he had to eat cheese sandwiches for lunch and dinner, rice crispies for breakfast. On that count, he relished the long eight hour drive back to Layton each weekend, where he could revel in the cooking and glorious food that Catherine whipped up for him with *love.*

Elvis tried as best he could to discover any staff at MB that were *abnormal.* He tried introducing in conversations in the lunch room, when there were diners, subjects allied to space travel and Sci-Fi stories about teleportation, just to see if anyone responded. Some did, but since Madame C's list didn't contain anyone remotely near San Diego, it turned out to be a futile effort, until a visiting engineer from New York flew in.

Frank invited Elvis to lunch with the VIP and himself. What a coincidence. But Elvis didn't carry around that list, so he couldn't verify if this was the same person. Nevertheless, he was going to try to steer the conversation towards his goal.

His name was Charles Lexington, very British sounding, and he was very British sounding. Seems he was responsible for the huge upswing in AM sales over the past few years, and MB snatched him with a very sweet five year renewable contract.

When Frank left for the rest room, Elvis asked Charles what past-times he enjoyed outside car engineering. Charles came back with gardening, tennis, cooking, paranormal and occult studies.

"Well, that's interesting, I have been studying in those areas too."

"You don't say. Seems everyone in the U.K. was into some kind of you know *out there* subjects. It goes back to before Shakespeare, witchery and sorcery and now UFOs and such."

"I'm more interested in UFOs and, ever hear of teleportation to other planets?"

"That's a bit far-fetched for me right now." But Elvis was close enough to detect that was not even vaguely true. "

"Yes, it is far-fetched, since no one has even come close to figuring out how it could be done."

"Oh, I'm sure it could be done," drolled Charles. "It's a matter of where you want to land with it. That's what makes it far-fetched to me."

"What if a person had a place they wanted to go, and not on Earth?"

"That would be interesting, indeed."

"You don't believe that an engineer of sufficient depth could bring it off do you?"

"As I said, it's peculiarity is not in the engineering of it but it's use. Once gone from this orb, there's no saying how the "subject" could return, see?"

"What if the subject didn't need to return?"

"Then that would be it, wouldn't it, and no one would ever know, much like death."

"The Bible has it that Enoch left earth and never returned. God took him to heaven is the passage."

"Wasn't aware of that, that's in the Bible you say?"

"And the fact that 900 foot giants roamed Earth at one time also."

Frank returned.

"Really elegant rest rooms here, they even have a valet with fresh towels and a shoe shine for 10 bucks."

"That's pretty routine in the U.K." And the conversation got back to design and specs and roll-out time tables.

Now Elvis had a comrade, at least one that could directly assist him, even if the comrade wasn't interested in traveling anywhere with it. When Elvis got back to his hotel room he found the list and on it he found the name Mr. R.C. Lexington, New York on it. 'God truly does help those who help themselves,' loomed largely in Elvis' mind as he got horizontal for the night.

C. Van Heyden

MANEUVERING

C. Van Heyden

By the second month, then late June, Elvis had stockpiled nearly a thousand dollars. He had carefully instructed payroll not to deduct anything since he was temporary, and had no job after summer, only college classes. So MB paid him as a contractor. He was tempted to buy a car for a $1000 and overall save on the monthly lease, but thousand dollar cars were notorious for going south or needing lots of repairs constantly. Charles had flown back to N.Y. the day after their lunch, and that meant it would be still longer before Charles would or could play a role in Elvis' departure from Earth. It looked that he would continue to follow his plan, and by end of summer, if he were not replaced sooner, assemble his funds and make plans for re-visiting the Turkish mountains.

Around this time, Elvis began experiencing difficulties with drafting the complex drawings fed him by Design. They had gone easy on him the first month, knowing that he was new, but the mistakes and they were not minor were coming back to him with request for corrections at a rate he was not accustomed to. If he got himself fired, well that was it then for the summer, and that would be another delay and problem. What was startling altogether was that Stockton hadn't come into his area at all to insult and degrade, and only now and then to Frank's. Elvis didn't have the cash free to pay Chuck or Rob to handle the intricate jobs or he would have. The only solution then was to put in more time on the weekends studying the manuals and texts on drafting. He stopped visiting Layton on the weekends. Catherine freaked when she heard Elvis say he's on the ropes at MB, and more so knowing he wasn't coming home, that wasn't the effect he wanted to create.

Since his motel was only four blocks from MB Design Center, Elvis got authorization to work on the weekends, and walked over to the main building Saturday and Sunday. All he had to do was sign in at the security desk after producing his ID card and sign out each day. He got to know the main guard so well he didn't have to show his ID most of the time. Having the shop to himself *without* the barrage of corrections to handle immediately he was able to teach himself the finer skills relating to three-dimensional modeling. It was one skill to design or draw an exploded view of a catalytic converter and a higher skill to model that in 3D on a computer.

Having within a few weekends taught himself the necessary skills to elevate his work to the quality demanded, Elvis was secure he would reach his target, reserving the extra funds he saved by not traveling back and forth to Layton, gas, food en-route and unnecessary car rental. By summer's end he had sequestered approximately four thousand dollars counting all expenses incurred, including a wardrobe, which he might even sell to a second hand men's shop that was nearby in Layton. Either way he had accomplished the major goal he set, something which was becoming more routine in his life.

Once home in September, and a little celebratory merry-making with Catherine out of the way, Elvis set to finishing his college year in one semester, while meticulously planning his next strategies. The only thing that interrupted the scene was a call from Frank saying that MB wanted him back and was willing to pay nearly double the salary.

What had happened was what happens more and more these days, people look good on paper but don't have the ability to deliver the goods or can't solve their own problems within the framework of a group, and the guy hired to replace Elvis bombed after two weeks leaving before he was terminated without notifying anyone. Despite that Bingham was piloting extension type courses for graduate and undergraduates, he declined since he had wanted to stay with MB no longer than was absolutely necessary.

So he resumed classes as usual, had to decline also again invitations to call the football scores for

Bingham game betters, and generally set his cap to look normal. He bumped into Olivia one day between classes and had quite a time maneuvering out of accepting her invitation to come over to her place for a meal, her modest exchange for his attention at the party. Finally he got himself cloistered enough to fend off those interruptions he was so used to getting every time he embarked on a major target he wanted to accomplish. He even enlisted the secretarial skills of Catherine, filtering incoming calls and messages through her, but not outgoing.

BHANGHI PASS

C. Van Heyden

Elvis knew his best course was to return to the Bhanghi Pass and the village at its base. If he couldn't accomplish contact with the overseers of the teleport he would make his way towards Fengcheng China and be completely earnest in his inquiries with Master Chip Ty Dick. He thought that he might detour to France and hook up with Mssr. Velatrobe, but he wanted very much to visit with Joshua soon. He missed his company.

By early December Elvis had enough credits to graduate with a Bachelor of Science in space engineering. The hardest part was telling Catherine he was going on a long tour again instead of starting work. Having grown so close and so fond of her, it would be gut-wrenching to leave Earth and to leave her behind. She would be devastated.

Retracing his exact steps he landed in Istanbul, contacted and rode in the same hired car to the village below the 10,000 foot location of the teleport. This time he wasn't carrying any of the climbing gear he brought on his first attempt.

He could not contact Bharabas for one last chance to capture some meaningful data from him. Bharabas had died. Ninety years old and no family to bury him. With the thought that his token could have been his passport to other worlds he went to talk with the town sheriff. The sheriff commiserated with Elvis but before his departure he handed him a small box, saying the old man had given it to him in case the *mountain climber* should return. But no matter Elvis would pierce the mystery in some way eventually by persisting if nothing else passed or no one came to help him.

Tactically the first target was to ascend the mountain and enter the hidden corridor early in the day, since previously he arrived late in the afternoon when the station was closing after a transfer occurred. He slept in the same hotel, even the same room. Early next morning he doused himself in the calendula and aloe lotion trusting that it would stick to him when his skin became the feathers of a falcon. His perception was always greater when transformed, but seeing feathers blacken would be too late a sign to escape, unlike the red prickly spots on human skin. As far as noise levels, he would take his chances knowing that the tympanum of a bird, the target organ receiving the intense vibrations, was a great deal smaller than a human one and thus less likely to be disturbed as much.

As he reported it to me: "I flew direct to the spot where the hidden entrance was concealed behind the narrow cleft in the granite peak. As I flew toward the inner cavern I felt the building of noise and the vibrations around my wings became so great I found it difficult to maneuver. Arriving inside the main transhipping area I perceived several large containers being hoisted through a portal that led to a much larger cube. This meant the return trip and that I had already missed the incoming freight and transportees who must have been quickly ushered down those long hallways and into a safe reception space. From there they most likely took elevators and tunnels within the mountain to exit in the village in some secret manner or in the low hills where concealment and debouche were achieved in thickets or behind outcroppings."

At this point in his report Elvis looked at me queerly. I thought he was going to say something like, "And then I spotted an overseer and was able to make contact." But he didn't. Instead he continued saying he would have tried to follow the halls and tunnels to see where they lead but he was unsure he could find his way back, and they might be as contaminated with radioactive material as the main chamber. He was at an impasse again, like before and had little time to figure out what to do. If this was in fact his ultimate means of salvation, it was simultaneously his nemesis now. Short of hiring a helicopter to airlift him in a hazard suit he could not establish a safe beachhead within shot of the control room or drone living quarters. With the force field surrounding, even that method was a long shot of getting back and safely inside again.

"And so I departed, flew back to the hotel, and changed back."

This last failure left Elvis completely down and out. He had had it well planned for success, and that he would finally come to grips with his urge to get back to Sellier and set things right. He was tired of *trying*.

The die was cast and once he landed in Istanbul Elvis flew to Beijing and then road the train to Fengshan province, and from there to the hotel in Fengsheng. It left him enough to live in town for a month, long enough he expected to attain what he came for originally. He was set and sure that he would confront Master Dick, not through a via but directly and he would confess completely his intentions to him.

RECONCILIATION

C. Van Heyden

It had been six months since Josh's last letter which told of his success in building the new home for his master. It seems that Josh also had accelerated his ability to learn and his ability to handle his duties in the year and a half since they had parted. What would it be like to get the full story from a master of Tae Kwan Do and obviously a superior being in other regards. This occupied most of Elvis' thoughts and musings as he approached the hamlet four miles from the compound. All was as he left it, the hotel, the book store, the early risers at the hotel sipping white tea and enjoying succulent rice with scrambled eggs. Nobody lifting a head when he came down from his room, the same room as his first stay. The manager was as happy to see him as before, and asked if he wanted to extend his stay as before. But Elvis declined saying he needn't economize this time on expenses. Once again Elvis experienced a palpable somewhat misty nostalgia for China and considered how he would probably choose, as Joshua had, to live here of all places, if he had not already resolved to right an injustice elsewhere in the cosmos.

Finally, he decided and made the four mile trek to the new house to meet Master Dick. When he arrived, the old house was gone. Only the new home was visible and compared to the previous it was a mansion. The hedges were still there but cut down from their height of eight feet to about five. Did this mean Master Dick was through being the recluse, through with his security watch over his compound? Would he be easier to approach now because he had an able pupil proving that he was still a great teacher—that he had chosen well his acolyte, and made him into the best Tae student he could be.

Master Dick warmly welcomed Elvis, as he had previously. This time it was early afternoon and Joshua was busy with his exercises in the dojang.

"It is a pleasure to see you again," Master Dick announced as he put forth his hand in the American gesture.

"Am I interrupting?" While Elvis took the master's hand and shook it firmly.

"Not in the least. How do like what you see? You know Joshua has done well by me, and I'm satisfied with the new accommodations he's constructed."

"I think it is one of the most elegantly designed houses I've yet seen. And the town is as lovely as it was when I stayed there previously. You should know that if I hadn't made other plans, I would settle in this area of China for life."

"It is a way of life not well understood and consequently not appreciated by westerners, but I perceive that you are not as the bulk of them are. Tell me about your plans, won't you?"

"Indeed, you have perceived me correctly, and that alone is comforting in a foreign land. But not very foreign now that this is my second visit."

"Joshua hinted that you had experienced some failure that was particularly distressing to you, is that why you are here again?"

"Right again Master Dick. It is that exact occurrence which has lead me back to Fengsheng and to your home. When I was here before I tried to find out the extent of your skills and powers without revealing why I wanted to know. Now, I will tell you why."

"Please come in and sit in the study while I heat a pot of white tea, you do drink it yes?"

"Of course, it is a delicacy for me, since it is practically unknown where I live."

"If it is all right with you I can hear you well in the kitchen, can you likewise here my voice?"

"Clearly."

"Then why not go ahead and tell me why you want to have this information."

"Joshua at one time was my confessor at college. He may have told you of his reversal of goals, of his coming to realize that his most cherished desire in life was not to minister to others, but to attain a high mastery of martial arts. And it was because of my abilities, and my familiarity with my own goals that I was able to free him from his misdirected life."

"I perceived him to be completely honest in his approach, and that is why I accepted him as a pupil, even though I had retired from teaching."

"Precisely, and when Joshua informed me of your methods of instruction and some other practices, I became curious, very curious about your knowledge and powers. Enough so that I used what funds I had left to travel six thousand miles to meet you personally. You see, my goal is to leave Earth and to acquire existence on another planet very distant from Earth named Sellier. A planet from which I was barred and expelled for crimes alleged that I did not commit. In Earth years quite a long time ago."

"Go on please."

"Since the time Joshua helped me to see my own misdeeds, my powers as a being have increased immensely, and by now you may know that I can change my shape. I can assume the shape of a falcon or other winged creature or even a quadruped if I need or desire. I can also detect, at short distances, what other beings are thinking, or trying not to think, and I can predict when absolutely necessary the future. My powers of mental concentration and observation have increased perhaps three times what they were a year and a half ago."

"I see, very impressive."

"I have used these powers to aid police to apprehend a pair of murderers, a band of bank robbers, and to free others as I have freed Josh from paths in life that they would never follow to conclusion successfully. But even with these powers, I have not yet found a way to return to Sellier, and to right the extremely unjust exile to Earth."

"You believe that I may assist you in this endeavor with my knowledge and abilities?"

"That is why I have traveled *more than* six thousand miles again. I traveled here via a location in Eurasia where I was able to discover the presence of extra-terrestrials and a teleport where these type of beings regularly make visits and transport cargo to and from Earth. But I was not successful in reaching these beings in a way where I could be included in the utilization of their service. That was what distressed me."

"I see very clearly your angst and your disappointment. It is true that I have as you do the power to transform my physical being to that of a fox or other creature as I desire. I choose fox mainly since it is emblematic of wisdom and has been through the ages."

"And I a falcon, which is and has been a symbol for freedom, a free powerful and graceful bird, a hunter. But to no avail. I sense that I am marooned here on Earth."

"We certainly all come from different parts of the universe, of this I am sure. I imagine that in a year or so I would teach or better I would as you have rekindled in Joshua the knowledge that you speak of now. And it is right that one should clean his spirit as you have done through confessions, for spiritual knowledge is of no use to one who is burdened with misdeeds, if such a person can even comprehend that knowledge and truth."

"So, you do have reality like mine?"

"I know that I have lived many lives prior to this one, in different locations and in different forms."

"Do you know where your last form was before Earth?"

"That information is not available to me."

"For myself, I was a rebel leader on Sellier, and I was accused falsely of crimes for which I was exiled to Earth."

"And some of your powers are from that period of time, I presume."

"By carefully examining my actions since and confessing the bad ones I have regained some but not all of those powers."

"And you are needing—you are looking for others who may have likewise been exiled in order to get back?"

"That has been my preoccupation for the last two years."

At that moment Master Dick fell silent and pondered.

Elvis wanted something momentous to transpire. He waited for Master Dick to speak again. It seemed to him that his entire life was held in suspension. 'No matter what comes now, I will not give up,' kept echoing in his mind.

"I believe that what you are really trying to do is right a grievous wrong, and that if you could stay here on Earth and yet somehow achieve justice back on Sellier you would be satisfied, is that so?"

"But, I don't have any reason to stay here if I can return."

"Don't you? There's at least Joshua, and he tells me that you are engaged to be married, there's that to consider."

"If I succeed in locating or developing a method of returning, I would take Catherine and Joshua with me, I would teach them what I know."

"But you presume that they would also have a strong desire to change civilizations, as you do, correct? And they may not have."

"I can live without them."

"But can you live with them? If they go only to please you or only because they feel indebted to you for the knowledge they have attained, then *they* would be *marooned* on Sellier, no?"

"I will find a way to go and come back, that they may have a choice which I did not have."

"But you say that you lead a revolt and a group of rebels who killed the agents of The Almighty? Were you not in effect doing things which should have gotten you exiled anyway?"

"Did Joshua tell you that?"

"I quickly gleaned what must have occurred from the generic story he told me from his life on Sellier. That story has repeated and repeated through the ages."

"What I did was wrong, but not indefensible."

"And what you have done up to now is right, and for that reason I will do what I can to help you."

"Great, then you do know how to travel to other planets?"

C. Van Heyden

"I do not, but I will help you nevertheless."

C. Van Heyden

THE RACE TO PERU

C. Van Heyden

The first thing Master Dick did for Elvis was to lend him a large sum of money, knowing that he had spent his entire reserves to get to China. Master Dick, he told Elvis, could live practically without assistance from anyone, with his vegetable garden and proximity to lakes for fishing. So, with his stipend from the state he was able to put away each year approximately five hundred dollars which he occasionally used to buy a new blender or other appliance as they gave out. It was out of this fund that the supplies for his new home derived. He'd been assiduously saving for twenty-five years. His only pay back was to be informed accurately of Elvis's findings if he should succeed.

The first step Elvis took was to try to reach Serena Amparo in Peru. He did not feel confident that he could find her quickly if he first travelled there hoping to locate her home, not knowing the language nor the country. But he was certain that visiting her was much preferred over South Africa, since that area where Gingham was, was known for the sudden breakout of hostilities and much drug trafficking. He made several calls to reach her hoping that she at least spoke a bit of English and understood it well enough for him to communicate to her why he was wanting to see her. Here again Master Dick allowed him to call long distance as he needed to, to make preparations.

After several calls to the village of Santa Miraflores, he found her number. Serena spoke halting English but enough that Elvis could understand her and she barely him. Serena understood exactly what he was after. She agreed to meet with him in two weeks' time or sooner if he could get to Miraflores earlier. She sounded old, but he didn't ask.

Elvis informed Master Dick that he had made contact and that he was scheduling the first flight out of Beijing International. Then Master Dick really surprised him—by informing him that he would personally chauffeur him to the airport. How? In his '51 Bugatti. What on earth thought Elvis. The Master had this exotic car stashed in a flaptrap barn like building, so no one would find it or even think to look there. Gorgeous two-seater that could fly on 8-cylinders of thrust. The Master knew much faster roads than the ones Elvis used to reach Fengsheng village by rental. The journey would take a day instead of two to three. The airport had only one flight per week to Brazil. Elvis would have to go via Sydney which was longer but faster. Shanghai had delayed service to Brazil and none to Peru. On top of all he gave Elvis a code that only he knew to get a sizable discount on his airline ticket. The master had been awarded this by China Airlines years ago for instructing two of their security guards in Tae, and they had in turn taught many more airport guards those skills.

There was barely enough time to talk with Joshua, to tell him he was off before fully arriving. Josh was not shocked. He knew how important and necessary was Elvis' desire to settle accounts back on Sellier. He hugged and wished him much success. The entire camp would be his to guard and to utilize while Master Dick was away. This Josh had earned.

C. Van Heyden

SERENA AMPARO

C. Van Heyden

Arriving late at night, after two days en route, Elvis sought shelter and the next morning his rendezvous with Serena. When they first met, he was taken a bit by how small she was and delicate. He knew Peruvian women as were most Latin women petite, but she was almost child-like, yet clearly not a child. He had bought and brushed up on as much Castilian Spanish that he could learn in 48 hours. So, when he came into her presence he was ready to parley.

"Buenos días senorita Amparo. Soy, Elvis Apolliani."

"Encontada, señor. Soy *Señora* Amparo."

"Perdón. Senora. Permítame usar *Serena?*"

"Sí. Está bien."

"And now, since I speak little Spanish, as I know you know, may we converse in English?"

"Sí. But I not speak good English, you know."

"Yes, but I know less Spanish than you English."

"OK."

"I am so thrilled to know what you told me on the phone."

"You mean about the flying saucers?"

"Exactly. I think I may have finally gotten to the place on Earth where I shall succeed the best. Is it true that you have spoken with them?"

"Yes, I have spoken, in so many words. And you will also, I'm sure."

"Where do we meet them?"

"They come and go almost regularly. I will show you the place."

At this moment, Elvis was electrified that he was about to meet and communicate with beings that no doubt had access to vehicles that went anywhere they wanted to go. But he couldn't go directly to them, he had to wait for them to come down and visit first. When he asked Serena what they looked like, she only said, "like me." Now he knew they would not be the same beings he witnessed working at the teleportation plant. Plus those beings probably were only able to transport him back to their planet or planets but not Sellier, since a plant would have to have been established there also.

Serena showed him a large field, fairly flat, which was their favorite landing zone. Her house was only a few hundred yards away. Serena invited Elvis to stay at her house. He accepted.

In many ways, the mien and manners of his host resembled those of Master Dick. She prepared a Peruvian dish for him, that was a favorite in that region called Seco—a stew which is the opposite of its meaning, dry, in Spanish. They talked about the town nearby and the life she had led in it for the many years. They talked while the lamb and casaba, with rice and pinto beans, red onion, lime, cilantro and peppers simmered. Then, when they sat down to dine, she told Elvis that, "They are very curious about this planet." And further, "They, many theys, have been coming here for a very long time." Here it became difficult to understand her. So she called a neighbor over to translate.

This neighbor a man, quite old, but alive as any person Elvis had yet met on his journeys, translated, "It had and has been and was a stopping place before launching outward to the other galaxies since Earth is so close to the rim of this galaxy."

"My desire is to hire them to take me back to Sellier

where I was expelled with no trial for crimes I did not commit."

"What will you pay them with?" translated the old man.

"I don't know right now. You say that they come and go regularly—perhaps they have not got what they are looking for, and I can help them find it or get it. You say they are not violent beings, right?"

"They have never hurt me or threatened me," continued the translator for Serena.

"And you say that *you* can easily accept their thoughts and they can yours?"

"I have never questioned it, so it remains mine to serve me or others like yourself," continued the translator.

"Then I will chance meeting them, with you of course."

The translator broke off his services at that moment and told Elvis that he would assist there also, since he had been with Serena on more than one occasion when the aliens came down.

Elvis was elated, a bit fearful still because of stories, more like rumors that because these beings were from another world they would treat us as animals or *aliens*, and that meant they would not do things to benefit us as they might their own kind. Wouldn't we treat them as specimens to probe and interrogate? was what he told me was uppermost in his mind.

Elvis decided he would further accept Serena's hospitality and stay with her but only if she accepted funds in exchange. She reluctantly accepted, such is the innate humanity in such a person.

The next several days Elvis tried to learn more Spanish, so that in the event that the old man was not available or, perish the thought, died between now and the appearance of aliens, he would have a better understanding of what the aliens needed to assist him. It was very hard since his head was full of conjugations not spoken Spanish, that his middle school teacher Ms. Tint enforced on him for three years in a row.

After a few weeks, while helping Serena harvest the fruit from the small orchards on her farm, he was able to grasp the simpler Spanish phrases. Her husband, he learned indirectly, had died in a local political skirmish and was buried in one of the orchards, which was her deceased husband's last request.

He became more confident of success, so much so that he wrote Josh and Master Dick that he could see the future coming and all his efforts coming to a glorious close in the remote Peruvian village.

There was one small problem left.

FOX AND FALCON

SAUCER BOYS

C. Van Heyden

What if the saucer beings didn't know how to get to Sellier? They must know. But where was Sellier? All that Elvis knew was that it was in the constellation Boötes and he could point the direction. But how far. Space travel required coordinates—exact coordinates. Which also included exact distances. Their attempt could be off by one tenth of one arc second and ten light years, spending an eternity searching in the wrong region of space. It's one thing to take off for a destination on a planet that's populated, where one can ask directions of natives or call home for backup and a complete impossibility to be out amongst the stars with no exact map or matrix. That's not how Elvis predicted his return as a revenant would play out. This was something even Madame C. could not deal with.

But the idea next that mushroomed up in his mind was that of R. C. Lexington, the engineer. The engineer that said to him, "It's a matter of where you want to land with it. Its peculiarity is not in the engineering of it, but it's uses," speaking of a teleportation device. And Elvis remembered very clearly hearing his thoughts, that as an engineer he didn't *truly* believe teleportation was impossible. Therefore he wouldn't *truly* disbelieve in extraterrestrial visitations and transportation devices. Elvis knew that such a visitation was imminent, he knew just as he knew who the bank robber was in San Antonio, and just as he knew which team would win the football game and by how much margin.

Elvis had not kept his number or an address. All that he knew is that MB Design had bought out his contract with AM, Aston Martin Motors? He called their head office, it was near 6:00 PM London time. Elvis got the security guard to stop the personnel director from leaving the parking lot and come back and take the call. When the director said, "Can't this wait until Monday I want to go home for the weekend?" Elvis turned up the intention.

"It is a matter of life and death that I reach Mr. Lexington tonight."

"You say you're calling from where, Peru?"

"Yes, and in less than a day or so my world will forever change for the worse if I don't reach him."

"Well, I've already missed dinner.... Let me see, no telephone number but a forwarding address in New York City for any monies and share liquidation he was owed."

Taking the prized address and after hanging up to London, Elvis dialed information in New York and asked for his number by address. None listed.

'Damn,' thought Elvis 'I've got to reach him.'   He put on his sweetest manners and asked a gigantic favor of the operator.

"Can you please give me three numbers of addresses close to his?"

"I shouldn't do it, but I will this one time."

Elvis took and called one after the other. No go. He repeated his entreaty twice more with two more operators. On the ninth call he got a person who knew R.C Lexington and his bloody number as well! Elvis had to leave a message. He left a *very* good one.

C. Van Heyden

LEXINGTON & CASSANOVA

C. Van Heyden

In getting prepared for the inevitable meeting when the UFO riders made their way back to Santa Miraflores, Elvis kept at it studying Spanish, as many hours as he could take, which wasn't many since he flunked it in middle school and disliked his teacher in spades. Serena was the key and the weak link because she spoke so little English, and the idioms in Spanish always threw him, just like our sayings throw foreigners when they arrive stateside. The word *porque* means both *why?* and *because*, how does that make sense? Well it does if one realizes that the answer to the question is the same question only in reverse, and by pronouncing "porque" faster it means because with the accent on the "por" and not the "que". Even if the old man wasn't sick when the aliens arrive or dead, he might not know how to say in English technical words or technical phrases that engineers and astronomers use, not to mention what saucer fly-boy aliens parley. So, Elvis kept it up and tried to talk to Serena in her language as much and as often as he could, while helping bring in the modest fruit harvest each day. He thought that she must be lonely without a husband, then dismissed that thought. She was happy with her life and she had a long life ahead of her, possibly a very long life, since who knows what she had learned from the visitors. She seemed quite young in appearance, though very petite.

A call came in from R.C. and when Elvis answered, R.C. said, "You've been looking for me?" somewhat surprised.

"I have, and I much appreciate the return call. Remember we talked over lunch for a while about things like the occult and paranormal phenomena?"

"Yep, I remember. You were telling me about teleportation, and then said something about Enoch and 900 foot giants Yea, I do, is that what you called so urgently for?"

"Sorry, no, that's not it. But it is paranormal. I'm here living with a person who has met and communicated with aliens, and many times. These aliens she says come down regularly and she has an ability to reach them and they her without moving the mouth."

"So, you want me to what?"

"I need your engineering background to locate a planet named Sellier and tell me the spatial coordinates."

"Do you know approximately where it is?"

"Yes, but not exactly or the exact distance, which is why I called. If I draw a map of the sky at night and place an arrow going to the destination of that planet can you get a much closer set of figures?"

"Well...I don't think I'm qualified to do it, but I do have colleagues who can."

"What would you want, or they want in exchange?"

"I don't know. What are you doing with the data?"

Elvis knew it was time to spill the beans, even if it meant Lexington's derision.

"I'll lay it out flat and plain. I want these aliens to take me there."

"I see, and how will you get back?"

"I'm not coming back, it's one way."

"I see." There was a long pause. "I have a friend who is an astronomer named Casanova, and he could do the deed, I'm pretty sure. Send me a fax, and make it very clear, marked exactly and with all that you know of it."

Elvis sighed deeply but away from the mouthpiece.

"I can't ever repay you of course, because I won't be here anymore if this works."

"Well, for Mr. Casanova, perhaps a short report on the aliens would suffice."

"Yea, that I could do. I could write it quickly and give it to Mrs. Amparo here, the contact and go-between and she could fax that when she goes into the city again."

"I'll get back to you when I have the data, but be sure you are sure before you send it."

"Right...I'm sure and have been for a long time."

GETTING READY
TO DEPART

C. Van Heyden

At the same time Elvis was joyful again, he was sweating bullets, considering how intricate this journey could be, and if he got lost why that would be it, wouldn't it? He'd wind up committing suicide probably as it was not likely he could live with the aliens on their planet and why would he want to? Holy guacamole, he didn't have any idea if he could stand space travel in a saucer, he didn't have a space suit or an oxygen breathing apparatus. God, this could turn into a debacle for sure.

Elvis started keeping a diary so that all the events leading up to and including his departure would be recorded for Mr. Casanova, for Lexington, for Catherine and Josh, and even for posterity, because even though Elvis didn't belong here he had lived here and to that degree he was tied to the inhabitants.

When he told Serena that he needed to send a fax and why she understood. That night Elvis spent most of it wrapped in a blanket studying the heavens. Waiting for the time to be the same as when the séances took place only he knew he had to account for the huge difference in latitudes or else he would give Lexington bum data.

The next day Serena drove into town and there he made out, using a ruler and colored pens an exact picture of where he knew the planet Sellier was located, in Boötes, and he was able to use two *close* stars flanking where Sellier was that for sure Casanova would recognize. Then the wait.

- - -

While Elvis was waiting, he received a telegram from Josh. It read that he was impressed and gladdened that Elvis' long planned and sought return pilgrimage to Sellier was at hand. He further stated that Master Dick had found in himself a worthy successor, and because the master had no living relatives to take his position upon death, that he would be honored if Josh would accept being appointed his beneficiary. This left only Catherine. To her Elvis sent a passionate letter explaining some of the mysterious vagaries of their relationship, the trips to Europe and before, and told her he has been immeasurably happy being her steady. He sent it knowing that very likely by the time she received it he would no longer be marooned on Earth.

PART III

SELLIER

C. Van Heyden

SELLIER

Sellier is a planet that doesn't forget. Its inhabitants remember perfectly their past and their past lives. So, when Elvis returns finally, he is right where he wants to be to vindicate himself, while revealing the evil things he did that he was not caught for and punished.

And while he's actively setting the score straight, he meets a woman who is strangely very much like Catherine, only Catherine isn't on Sellier. She is back on Earth!

When Elvis Apolliani finally met with success in Peru, with the help of Mrs. Amparo, hooking up with the flying saucer aliens he had decided he would not press Catherine nor myself to go with him, back to his home planet. He rightly knew that if we, Catherine and I, didn't fit in there was no way really for us to return to Earth. So, Elvis met the alien spacecraft flyers, and with the help of and her ability to harvest thought from them, got them to agree to take Elvis to Sellier. But in return they wanted something that they perceived he might have, when he told them of the transshipment area he had invaded to find a way back. It was the token that Bharabas (BHAR-AH-BAS) had left him as a memento as much as a talisman. The token that symbolized the technology of teleportation, a technology the fly boys, from who knows where, didn't have. This he related to me, Joshua, in a letter quickly jotted on a piece of stiff cardboard that was handy.

Later, and I still don't know how, Elvis was in touch with me, I would call it one-way "long-distance telepathy". Naturally he told me to convey this also to Catherine. Here is what he told me.

SELLIER

TAKE OFF

C. Van Heyden

I boarded the space craft (saucer like) with the indispensable help of Serena (Mrs. Amparo), who did a bang-up job of interpreting the alien speech / telepathy to me and mine to them. The child-like* aliens were jazzed about the token I showed them and on that alone decided they could trust me. Since I had no suit, and wasn't built like them, which was as far as I could perceive a rubbery plastic type body, they put me in a coffin type apparatus which was pressurized and even had oxygen which they needed very little of themselves. I was relieved to find out that they didn't have to freeze me, just protect me from the pressure changes. I have to admit when these flyboys first landed I was *very* apprehensive as to the outcome since they being from, jeez, another part of the universe they couldn't possibly have any respect for other planetary life forms, knowing how invaders and explorers usually are. As far as I could tell the ship wasn't armed with any weapons, but then nobody was firing on them or attempting to drag them off somewhere for interrogation. Something, although, told me that if I crossed them or attempted any more than being just a passenger they would make me regret it. I wasn't one of them and never would be.

Now, here's the real great part: when I showed them the star map that Lexington prepared for me for them, they showed more interest and they told Mrs.

Amparo they knew where this place (Sellier) was. Man that was the best news ever! I almost got the feeling that they liked me. That was the other piece of news which convinced me that I would trust them and go with them. But when I asked them how long? *to get there* the interpretation came back garbled even to Serena, but I didn't care. I was going no matter what.

 When Serena and I had hugged I handed her my letter to Catherine and said goodbye. I was escorted onto the ship and immediately we took off. I felt a little vulnerable. Once in the pressurized unit I could hear nothing and see only the dark grey ceiling above me. The only reason I asked how long? was that even though these saucers were known to dart around fantastically fast, I still believed that stars were so far as to make journeys between them very long, and I would get very hungry if I didn't eat. Even this Serena was able to fathom to the aliens, although I get that they probably, since they had visited Earth many times before, knew already I had an animal type body that needed nourishment regularly. In a matter of minutes I was hooked up to what on Earth would be called an intravenous, only this one went directly to the stomach and was very pleasant, amazingly. I even got the sensation of muscle movement from some external source, so I concluded that I was not the first human or animal body they had transported. We were en route.

SELLIER

ARRIVAL

C. Van Heyden

338

Josh, we've arrived! This is so SO incredible. I recall this place like it was only yesterday. Beautiful too. Let me explain. On Earth there was once a civilization called Atlantis, a very, *very* advanced type civilization. Well this planet Sellier, at least where the aliens dropped me is a whole lot like the mythical Atlantis, don't ask me how I know. Populations back on Earth would be astounded to see what I am seeing, and to know that they are not alone, not even close. You know, because I took you through some of your bad times here, remember? But for every bad time there are many, many good times. After all that commotion, revolution, purging, violence and murder I am looking at...well god if only you could see what I am seeing. Perhaps I can send an image as well as my word thoughts. (But he couldn't, so he described Sellier to me.) First of all the daylight is very much like Earth, and the air, yes air. I wasn't so sure that would be what I found, is practically the same, but definitely sweeter and purer. And the land, at least where I am looking, is all beautifully terraced and verdant and lush and there's so much of it. I haven't seen any water, but I'll bet there's oceans or enormous lakes.

There are some peculiar towers placed around in a circle but very pretty, like tall pagodas. And there are roads, and trees with very smooth and very hard bark. There are even flowers! This is just too amazing. Some object just flew overhead at phenomenal speed and disappeared over a low mountain. Guess they have airships. I don't remember them, but I was sent off in something like a rocket when I was exiled. Those aliens were very smart to drop me away from any *seeing eyes.* It may be that if I parachuted in, this is funny, I would wind up a specimen on my own true planet. I'm going to stop transmitting for a while until I locate and figure out a good way to introduce the fact to the citizens that I've returned. Note: How Elvis knew when to reach me in waking hours, I cannot right now explain.

Several hours passed: I'm looking at Greco-Romanesque type building and now I know that I AM home. This is what I remember so well. There are people thronging this modest city shall I call it, don't know, have nothing to compare it to. But I have met one inhabitant so far who stopped to converse with me, and I could tell from their expression they knew I was from not their area. He or she, can't tell quite yet, everyone looks so healthy and vital, all wearing loose fitting clothing of some thin lightweight material. Oh, I forgot to mention the temperature is mild, get that. It is so natural like back in Peru I didn't even realize it, unlike the times I stepped off planes in China and found the heat unbearable. I'm still wearing my jumpsuit which is getting some pretty strange looks from time to time. Must be the wrinkles from lying "in state" for so long ha-ha. Never did find out how long the trip from Earth to Sellier was. I don't know what they eat, should say what *we* eat, now that I'm stranded back on my planet. Judging from the general body types I would say food like back on Earth, but I have a sneaking suspicion it leans toward fruits and vegetables; there's no one so far that has an ounce of fat on them.

And then Elvis quit transmitting for a while.

C. Van Heyden

SELLIER

CATHERINE

C. Van Heyden

Back on Earth, Catherine was struck dumb when she read Elvis's letter. She told me that she had no idea. Catherine in her naïveté believed everything, all the white lies, Elvis told her, but I assured her he was not lying about having loved her for the time they were together, this I was sure of as Elvis had confided this fact to me more than once.

When she read the part of how Elvis had wanted her to come along with him, but he was very hesitant knowing it would be a one-way, she cried. She told me, "I would have gone, I trusted him. Wherever he wanted to go I would've have gone, even to another planet." Then she got angry. "Damn it Joshua. He didn't even give me the choice." I could say nothing to console her. I too, felt left out. And now that he had succeeded, I even wished to hell he had invited me, even though I committed to be Master Dick's beneficiary and estate holder. I at least had some knowledge of his planet, in fact Sellier was once my home also.

Catherine thought of telling her father Frank that she had been abandoned, but rescinded the idea. I was able with Master Dick's financial help to make a voyage back to the U.S. to be with Catherine, as it was Elvis' last desire and instruction. In any other situation I would have done much the same as brothers do for each other when one goes off to war and dies, and the other takes on the responsibilities for the widowed wife, even though Catherine was not a widow technically. We spent many times together until I could stay no longer and returned to Fengcheng and my place supporting Master Dick. It was a few weeks after I arrived back in *my new home* that Elvis started broadcasting, so that may tell readers how long it took between planets. Master Dick was so pleased to hear of the success of Elvis' daring attempt. He said nothing more on the subject ever again.

SELLIER

REGALLIA

C. Van Heyden

When next I received messages from Elvis he had met and *spoken* with an inhabitant of Sellier and this is what he told me.

Josh, you won't believe it, but I've met a girl...a female, a woman, she's gorgeous and so intelligent and she's a lot like Catherine in many ways! (Boy, was Elvis excited.) The women here all wear their hair short, like the page boy look but much prettier. Her name is Regallia. She is of marriageable age, she told me right out. Apparently, sex is not so hidden and manipulated on Sellier. She's a very bold person in her occupation. Seems she is an engineer by trade, but one who is hired by companies to seek out rich deposits of minerals, especially uranium. Well paid, and when I told her who I was SHE REMEMBERD ME! SHE REMEMBERD MY BEING EXILED. SHE REMEMBERED HER LIFE AT THE TIME OF THE UPHEAVAL AND DEPOSING OF THE ALMIGHTY AND THE CONSEQUENT DEMISE OF THAT WORLD. (At this point I thought my head was coming off so rambunctious were his thoughts coming through very strongly and he continued:) MY FRIENDS ARE STILL HERE! MY FRIENDS ARE STILL HERE!! (Then nothing) I thought he was going to drop unconscious from the exertion. Then very slowly and very carefully he explained that on Sellier the inhabitants don't FORGET. They remember everything. That makes for a very safe and sane civilization. People don't do stupid or bad things ordinarily. They know that they will live again, and so no one can control them with fear or threats. (I hadn't thought of that.)

Elvis told me that they communicate with thought also, and he didn't *have to* learn Sellier's spoken languages because there were none, but they did have some, for signs and written materials. That's why he could read Stockton's thoughts and even my thoughts when he took me back to my life on Sellier; we weren't conversing with words, and I never knew it. I have that ability too, though partially developed, since I lived on Sellier.

Then things turned serious. Serious because, we both knew about the deeds he had done on Sellier that got him exiled, albeit for the wrong crimes. They *were bad deeds*. How could they have happened? Elvis didn't or couldn't explain that at all, but he vowed he would find out and give me what he found.

350

SELLIER'S HISTORY

C. Van Heyden

For the time being Elvis would enjoy being home; he would try to get a job or some work to support himself, and he would definitely court Regallia, or let her court him. That's more or less what happened he told me.

About this time, I started picking up that Master Chip Ty Dick wanted to go out peacefully from his mortal existence. I observed him carefully writing things into a diary of sorts, and carefully going around his acreage tending to the plants. He told me soon I would be fully in charge and we both bowed knowingly to each other. He also encouraged me to look for students and to take only the sincere ones. He had put an ad, unbeknownst to me, in the Fenshan weekly paper, and students began arriving to be interviewed. One such student reminded me of myself two and one half years earlier, and I agreed he would be my first pupil in the martial arts. Without a word of guidance from the Master, I began to educate my new pupil as Master Dick had educated me.

Now, returning to Elvis on Sellier. Seems Regallia discovered Elvis' facility for space engineering and his ability to dance, both of which interested her, and found him work with an allied firm that made those fast moving whatever they were flying devices he had glimpsed on first arriving. The dancing he didn't go into but I gathered the folks on Sellier dig it a lot and are usually quite good at it. I will admit, with the perspicacity of the inhabitants of Sellier I shuddered to think what they might do to Elvis when or if they found out what acts he had perpetrated there.

Apparently Regallia was not so much impressed that Elvis was a revenant as much as that he took the chance of hitching a ride with the alien space jockeys. She did not like them at all and told Elvis that he was a very lucky guy to have not been molested by them. She *was* going to have him get scanned for implants, but he sweet-talked her out of doing that, saying that he was awake the whole journey in a state of reverie much like when he would lie back in a summer hammock on a tranquil day and contemplate his future. And he messaged me thus.

I've been trying to learn from Regallia anything about *those days* when tyranny and counter tyranny swept Sellier. She told me that according to her recollection the main problem, the one that caused political discord was simply the stupidity of the governing bodies to deal with the population increase. They couldn't keep up with the demands for infrastructure without taking drastic steps to curb procreation, and this infuriated the populace, and allowed insurgents to rise who championed against those in power who advocated severe birth control and limiting family sizes. Now, that was a curse no longer because by necessity, out of the devastation from all that conflict came men, and some women who found ways and who developed technology for making inhabitable spaces habitable for people, for increasing the food supply, quite cleverly by the way, for improving the retention capability for students so they could graduate much earlier and have more to offer the work-a-day world in the bargain. Overall the atmosphere turned from solemn protective to nearly *vie libre*. Let people live. Trust them to do the right thing, without interfering. I told her in turn that I had been one who challenged the authority of leaders. She acknowledged that without comment.

Much of what I have learned from wise Regallia could be put to use by governing bodies on Earth to their mutual success. For instance, the complicated law system and the writing of enormously long bills that go on for hundreds even thousands of pages doesn't exist on Sellier. The limit on pages here is 100, and few bills ever reach that total. So lawyers don't abound here, whereas artisans are everywhere. As I said the need for law and order, much less police is undeniably superfluous; it just doesn't get that serious. Not that crimes don't ever occur. In fact, there was one just a few days back, and pretty heinous too, seems a man, a crazed man, took a machete type weapon and proceeded to chop up another man accused of seducing his wife away from him. Found out later, the guy was a married man with family and wasn't the guy he was after in the first place. What was the penalty? The man who did the chopping inherited the dead man's wife and children to support for life on his recommendation. Seems fair to me.

I don't know when I am going to reveal my crimes of the past, but it won't be long. It can't be, amongst very honest people it's rather painful withholding misdeeds.

SELLIER

THE QUESTION

C. Van Heyden

Elvis related an observation to me one evening early that I think is worthy of inclusion. There was on Earth an "Age of Reason" but there on Sellier it is an age of Aesthetics, and that is far more sustainable since it results in tangible products that support life, instead of "ologies" which have the tendency to support conflicts. I was still worried for Elvis' safety because of the potential reaction that lies beneath the calm exterior of most beings when memories of cruel times are reactivated. Remember his counter-vigilante group acted to hasten the demise of the Almighty and civilization as they knew it at the time. Even though many of the inhabitants there were capable artisans and artists, there were also many who made their living supporting them with the mundane tasks of existence and these beings had the ability to recall the past and their past lives. So even without a reaction they could well up as a force and destroy Elvis or put him on an interminable series of amends tasks.

So, Elvis decided he would confess all to his new love, Regallia, and see if she would understand. And as it turned out, in relating the details, he also touched upon the one murder he was truly ashamed of, Colton, and this had been Regallia's brother. But Elvis would not propitiate his death to Regallia, one, because he knew that she would take it as a weakness, and two, he was confessing, and this was not the time to make right the wrongs he committed. Instead he continued to right up to and past the time of his summons, accusal, imprisonment and eventual banishment from Sellier. This ended, Regallia asked him a question he dreaded hearing..."What will you propose to balance the acts you've committed when it comes time to report them to the authorities so that you can remain here with good conscience?" And this he did not know, so he did not answer.

SELLIER

EXPIATION

C. Van Heyden

When I finally communicated his transmissions to Catherine, she quickly proposed that I help her locate Serena Amparo, so she could go and join Elvis on Sellier. Then I had to explain quite at length that he had found a new love, and that even if I could locate Serena, there was no chance of repeating Elvis's success since he had very luckily the token they desired. This was the final crushing event for her.

The day finally came also when Chip Ty Dick, Taekwondo Master and my mentor left his mortal self. In a ceremony that dated back centuries, I and my new student wrapped the Master's body in silk bandages and carried it to the far extent of his property, and there in the evening burned the remains to ashes, as was his instructions. The next day the cold ashes were added to the berm for a blue lotus plant newly added to the garden the Master tended all his life. He left me complete instructions on mentoring students, on taking care of the grounds, and some vintage books on the Ramayana and other Hindu writings covering the skill of shape-shifting. I could not tell Elvis all that had transpired for I as yet was not adept as he in long distance telepathy, and anyway Elvis had his own problems to face on Sellier and would not countenance much anymore what happened on Earth, even to a *blood brother* of sorts.

While I took care of the proper disposal of Master Dick's body, Elvis had come upon a plan after contemplating how to soften the blow of his evil deeds when he revealed them to the people of Sellier, at least the city he knew as Sellier. He was not sure even his plan would be enough to keep him from being ostracized immediately to the inhabitable regions. He was sure to reveal all the tedious and degrading times he had spent on Earth and make sure his listeners would know that his exile was no dispatch to the isle of Elba.

As he told it: "I could not simply vow to never employ counter-vigilante methods again nor vow to always be a good citizen, that was already a given if you planned to live on this planet. What I could do is employ my powers to undo, at least as much of the chaos and death that remained residually in the collective psyche of Sellier from those horrendous times. As with my regressing of selective students back at Bingham University, I would take, on a non-paying basis, several citizens who were game to undertake a spiritual revisiting of those times with an aim to expunge all of or, most of the *shock* that hit them. Choosing randomly from only those citizens who by actual attestation new that their subsequent lives were tainted, even warped by the foment and sheer brutality they experienced. Never telling them or indicating that they would have to purge their souls too, to get full benefit. This is my plan, this is what I'll propose when I go before the council."

Elvis didn't know, if approved, if even he would live long enough to carry out the one-on-one *deep* counseling. But he stated to me emphatically that that was the very best contribution he could make. The Council met every six months, and that was fast approaching.

C. Van Heyden

SELLIER

MAKING ALLIES

C. Van Heyden

Elvis needed friends ahead of his confession; he needed to have that security since he planned on staying on Sellier and marrying Regallia and having children and doing what he planned, not only for citizenship but for his own conscience and integrity. With friends to support him, even if he should be denounced, he would have a better go of it certainly than with only Regallia by his side. So, Elvis made every effort to create positive feelings about himself. The first way was to repeat his successes with the students of Bingham University but on Sellier.

At work he found a co-worker who reminded him very much of Lexington back on Earth: suave, caring, well-educated but not the least snobbish. Elvis tells it this way: Alex worked near me in propulsion and I worked in...well design and mechanical drafting but not a novice position anymore. We are about the same height and weight and we lunch together, even though he has never known me on Sellier before. We seem to just like paling around, you know like when your kids and there's no status thing going on like later in life. He tells me all about the sub-orbital rocket ships that go everywhere, and I tell him about the new *secret designs* he's not to know about until released. I said earlier the air is noticeably fresher than that on Earth, and the reason is I found, there's slightly more oxygen and nitrogen and less hydrogen in it. The rocket fuel, classified data, burns more steadily and longer because of the higher nitrogen content. For the interstellar craft only nuclear reactor fuel is used. You know what that means? I could conceivably return to Earth someday. On the other hand I could be deported again.

I recently asked Alex if I were to be accused or even found guilty of a crime, albeit from *very* long ago, would he disown me? Alex thought about it for a moment and said, "I wouldn't disown you, because I know you, but I would, could only give testimony as to the good traits you've shown me." And when he had said that he asked the nature of the crime. This made me extremely uncomfortable because I didn't know whether he had been alive during that period, and I also didn't know whether I may have injured someone close to him or himself. He had never heard of The Almighty, and no recall on any planet-wide revolution. I wasn't in the clear even then because when I told him the nature of the crime he wanted details.

BEFORE THE
HIGH COUNCIL

C. Van Heyden

That night, as Elvis tells it, something about Alex's inquiry set things on end, and he once again had a terrible dream. "I was swimming in mucous, the world was full of mucous, Everywhere I looked trees, flowers, plants, mountains, valleys were covered with mucous. Animals too. I flew high as a falcon and I could see the deserts of Sellier dripping with mucous, the plains and even uninhabitable areas stuck in that yellowish viscous and slimy substance. Even the rocket planes and suborbital conveyances: all covered in mucous. The houses and homes the parks and festival areas deluged. The enormous lakes were covered with a bubbly, frothy mucous like the turbulent backwash of a filthy canal. Nowhere could I see a location that was not inundated. Even at the poles of Sellier, there it was. I looked with horror to the double sun and it was encased in a brownish muck."

When I finally awoke, I was sick. Very sick. I crawled out of bed and heaved a great wad of mucous into the disposal. I cannot wait another day. I'm going to the council chambers and ask for a non-scheduled hearing. If I am lucky they won't make me wait. I must relieve myself of these pressures.

With Regallia's influence, Elvis got a special audience with the council.

...

"Gentlemen and gentlewomen, I have come before you with this matter of urgency, utmost to myself, in great hopes that by confessing my misdeeds *and* by proposing a project to the council to set these matters to rest, I will relieve my troubled soul of their burden while achieving thereby the consent and goodwill of the council and all citizens of Sellier, that being the chief objective of the purging."

Given the nod to proceed by the head council member, I began the tale of The Almighty, his demise and my crimes attendant to that period. I left out nothing. I did not try to vindicate my actions in anyway, nor bring the subject of my exile and its painful details up except as sequential acts to all that came before. This time I was able to name each of the victims dispatched by the counter-vigilantes and myself, so that any citizen that was affected by or made uncertain as to why or how their comrades, spouses, brothers came to an ignominious end would be satisfied. When I was done there was commotion in the gallery. First, I perceived the thought, 'Banish him to the uninhabitable areas'. Another thought arose, 'What will you do to atone for your crimes?' And another from the dais, 'He should not be allowed citizenship nor the right to procreate.'

Regallia stepped forward and asked to be heard. This granted she eloquently began a defense for me against harsh punishment including the fact that as citizens we know how turbulent that time was in Sellier's history, and that there are few amongst us who did not commit crimes at that time worthy of censure if not severe punishment. However there were several in the gallery whose relatives were the targets of the murders, and they wanted reparations equal to the deeds. This the chairman heard and requested of me a direct response. I set out for all to perceive that I was contrite, that I was willing to attempt almost anything to achieve equality with them again short of debasing or degrading tasks, and that is when I launched the plan to alleviate the residual pain, that as citizens of Sellier knew, was inherent to life and to living through embattled times.

As I proceeded to relate my success on Earth with the technique first used with you, the gallery became noticeably less agitated. After finishing the details of how I would go about administering such contribution there was only one adversary. The one who wanted to deny procreation and marriage rights as well, even if I were successful. This then was a stalemate until Alex, unbeknownst to me in the gallery came forward with words of conciliatory effect. His argument was simple: He declared his knowledge of my worth, that I was capable of honest work and production, that I was trustworthy, and that I could have chosen to not reveal the crimes and simply lived amongst us *in cognito.*

I doubt that the enmity in the one council member was assuaged; nonetheless the council voted that my project be admitted for consideration but based on close scrutiny and testimony by the participants. But, if successful by report thereby, that the amends project be incorporated into my full existing lifetime and if possible taught to others who would or could use it for reconciling their transgressions with society. I was thanked for my confessions, as are all citizens who come forth for absolution, and in this I already felt more like one of the true inhabitants of Sellier than when I lived here before.

SELLIER

SENTENCED

C. Van Heyden

It made complete sense, after the hearing, that Elvis should deliver his *magical* beneficence to as many individuals as physically possible. He could of course also, after much success appeal the life term sentence to do this service, and the wise council would I'm sure agree. Either way he was conditionally accepted as a valid citizen again on his home planet, that being the entire objective of his confessions.

There was, according to Elvis's report, some scurrilous warnings posted anonymously around the city to scare inhabitants from accepting this *dubious service* as the posted handbills stated. But within a few weeks, the powerful effects of his abilities were overwhelmingly echoed by its beneficiaries, and the handbills disappeared for good. It was about this time, or maybe a few months later that I got a sudden transmission from Elvis and the nature of it made me shiver.

Those aliens that had dropped Elvis off many months earlier had come back. And they wanted something Elvis didn't want to give them. They wanted the location of the teleportation station on Earth, Elvis related. Apparently, this was only one of many visits to Sellier which is why they recognized how to get here from the map created by Lexington.

I perceived that they wanted to either capture, destroy or subjugate that outpost. I still could not communicate directly with them, but Regallia could which is why she despised them so much. As the discussion grew heated between myself, Regallia and the chief alien it appeared that they only wanted the technology at the station. From Regallia I got that this was a cover. Having no idea as to how the *other aliens* at the station would react, such as an all-out war I chose not to divulge its location. Then a most curious dialog emerged. The chief alien turned the conversation over to another alien who I presume was like to us a librarian. That alien began a very in depth and from what Regallia translated a very earnest plea for the information. The "librarian" stated time and place and form and event on every Earth war, major conflict, and civil commotion going back hundreds of years. Every assassination of a monarch or president and any country's leaders as well. The alien stated emphatically that the outpost station was in almost every case the feeder tube for instigators of these times of upheaval. In exchange for the location they would do their best to eliminate the outpost.

That was enough for me to act. My education at Bingham had taught me that wars were constantly being created to further one party's agenda or another, and most were started by religions for the main purpose to control populaces. I gave them what they wanted. Joshua, I want you to monitor the major military actions on planet Earth so that one day when you can reply to my transmissions you'll be able to corroborate or not what the librarian stated was fact. If the aliens are successful there should be a noticeable reduction.

C. Van Heyden

SELLIER

ENVOI

C. Van Heyden

In the second full year of Elvis' return to Sellier and cohabitation with Regallia, Elvis petitioned for reduction of sentence imposed and got a mitigated sentence, based on sufficient reports from citizens that he had helped to remove the stigma of those days when Sellier had gone to the dogs. His life was no longer pinioned to an interminable assignment. Justice had been served.

For myself, I did finally acquire the ability to telepathically communicate with Elvis, which is why those who have read these confessions can with complete confidence believe them and his story. And one more thing, and perhaps you may have also become aware of it, the outpost was destroyed. There have been fewer major conflicts since that occurrence.

C. Van Heyden

Does it take a Samson or Hercules to overthrow ones barriers and obstacles?

In ON CONQUERING THINGS the author both humorously and not so humorously tells of his subduings in life with stories of how conquering things *in life* is the main duty of a person, regardless of the odds.

Here is a rare and interesting glimpse into the fertile mind of a budding storyteller."
— Richard A. McCullough, The Rich Writers Coach™

Order via Amazon at Amazon.com

C. Van Heyden

All letters addressed to the author will be given immediate care and response. They can be addressed to:

Velvet Gloves Publishing
PO Box 17633
Nashville, TN 37217

Include a SASE

www.ingramcontent.com/pod-product-compliance
Lightning Source LLC
Chambersburg PA
CBHW061303170626
46817CB00001B/24